A Life in Three Octaves

DEEPA GANESH

A Life in Three Octaves

The Musical Journey of Gangubai Hangal

First published by Three Essays Collective in 2014

Published by Westland Non-Fiction, an imprint of Westland Books, a division of Nasadiya Technologies Private Limited, in 2025

No. 269/2B, First Floor, 'Irai Arul', Vimalraj Street, Nethaji Nagar, Alapakkam Main Road, Maduravoyal, Chennai 600095

ISBN: 9789360453626

10 9 8 7 6 5 4 3 2 1

Typeset by Digiultrabooks Pvt. Ltd
Printed at Thomson Press (India) Ltd

To Amma and Anna—
the centre of my universe

My gratitude to Babanna and Lalithakka
who took me into their fold like I was their own

Contents

Preface

It is eleven years since the first edition of *A Life in Three Octaves: The Musical Journey of Gangubai Hangal* was published in December 2013, her centenary year. This was four years after her passing away on 21 July 2009, at ninety-six. Memories flood me; in these fifteen years the world we live in has changed beyond recognition. At times, I even wonder if all these experiences were part of this lifetime.

As I have said in the book, there were set questions and set responses that you could expect from Gangubai. This can be easily attributed to old age, but it was also perhaps an exercise in revalidation. So many times, she asked: 'You will show me the book, won't you?' This was almost always followed by: 'But I can't read English properly.'

Gangubai didn't live to see the book.

Looking back, I know that this book could not have happened at any other time. Gangubai had stopped performing in public, and her daughter Krishna's death had thrown her musical life into a stillness. It was around this time that Manoj Hangal, *Ajji*'s beloved grandson, realised what a colossal loss it would be if her remarkable life went undocumented. It must be serendipity that his idea landed on my table.

When I embarked on the project, I saw that Manoj always had a clutch of ideas at hand—each time I met him, I was drawn into a new project, which would be followed by that other one, and then a subsequent third. Such ideas were constantly being distributed to his first circle of friends. However, if any of these ideas were realised, it was thanks to Manoj's execution. The most prestigious idea, fortunately, came my way: Project *Ajji*.

Exactly a decade after Gangubai's demise, on 15 May 2019, Manoj suddenly passed away at fifty-four years of age, due to acute diabetes. This was a very big blow to the family. All her life, Gangubai, her daughter Krishna, her son Baburao, his wife Lalitha and their four children had lived together. Manoj, the oldest grandchild, was a lawyer by profession. But he had given it up to take care of his grandmother. He never left Hubli and was always hovering around his *Ajji*. He, like his parents, was deeply concerned with preserving the musical legacy of Gangubai. He had set up the Gangubai Hangal Museum, collecting rare instruments from across the country and even abroad. He was talking to the government to take over her childhood home in Dharwad; he was organising concerts, for he believed in the dissemination and preservation of classical music. And there were many more things he did.

Manoj's demise shattered me. He was a rare human being—natural, spontaneous, impulsive, and generous to a fault. He had been my bridge to Gangubai, and all my memories with her are inevitably intertwined with Manoj.

His parents were inconsolable. But did they even get a chance to recover? In April 2021, Baburao, who had come to live in Bangalore with his wife Lalitha, called me. 'Something untoward has happened,' Baburao said. His daughter Vaishnavi and son-in-law Mahesh Talakkad had broken into their Hubli home, Ganga Lahari, which was also a museum containing priceless artefacts, awards, etc. They had done so without consulting the legal heirs, Baburao and Narayanrao, Gangubai's two sons. Baburao and Lalitha had moved into Arun's home in Bangalore during COVID and had to now be rushed to Hubli to look into the matter.

The ninety-year-old Baburao tried to convince his daughter, but in vain. Along with son Arun and older daughter Madhavi, he held a press conference in which he stated that it was the desire of the two brothers that the government take over Ganga Lahiri, the home of Gangubai, and also preserve the museum with its huge collection of instruments.

Three years have passed, and the government hasn't responded. Baburao, Lalitha and Manoj had lived all their life with Gangubai, attending to her till her last breath. Now Baburao can't even enter his own house. 'It is painful for me to see my mother's dignity maligned. I have tried hard. I don't know what the future holds,' he told me feebly. 'I have to face all this at this ripe old age.' Baburao, now ninety-three, is a sad man.

Exactly a month after the press conference in April, Madhavi succumbed to COVID in May 2021. How can I even explain the state of Baburao and Lalitha? They had lost two of their children, they couldn't go back to their Hubli home—the couple had become hostage to cruel times. Lalitha, too, passed away in 2023.

It was at Manoj's behest and relentless chasing that the government had allotted land for the Gangubai Hangal Gurukul, in Vidya Nagar, Hubli. The residential school, following the traditional gurukul model, was inaugurated in 2011 with six gurus and thirty-six students. After the initial years of smooth functioning, the annual funds were slashed by 60 per cent—from Rs 1.4 crore to 30 lakh. Finally, in 2023, reeling under a severe financial crunch, the administrative body of the Gurukul announced that if the government failed to release funds, it would have to stop functioning.

When the government declared its plans to merge the Gurukul with the Gangubai Hangal Music and Performing Arts University in Mysore, artistes all over the country, and connoisseurs, protested: it was the only Gurukul in India and it was on this land that Gangubai's *samadhi* had been built. The crisis is ongoing, still awaiting resolution.

In one of my initial meetings with Gangubai, she had complained that she didn't approve of the renovation of her house. She preferred the original style. The house was studded with memories of her daughter Krishna, guru Sawai Gandharva, uncle Ramanna, children, grandchildren … In any conversation, this would invariably come up. Ganga Lahiri meant everything to her, she had saved it with great difficulty.

Gangubai had carefully shed the social baggage that had been passed on to her. She desired that her children and the future generations of her family should live free of the adversities that she had known. From the way she planned and led her life, it almost seemed that she was keen on leaving a good life for them and not so much her musical legacy. Yet, fifteen years after her passing, everything seems to be at risk.

If I close my eyes, I can hear the chaos that the house loved so much. The constant stream of visitors, *Ajji*'s patient enquiries, the kitchen sounds, the free and easy nature of their hospitality, Baburao and Lalitha's high-pitched conversations, arguments, great-grandchildren—it is here that Gangubai, for decades, had entered into *riyaz*.

On a quiet afternoon or evening, when there were just a couple of senior students, Manoj would drop himself into a chair with a huge thud. 'Give me black one,' he would ask one of the students for the pitch. Breaking into one of *Ajji*'s celebrated renditions—Bhairavi, Miya Malhar or Yaman—as the day's fancy decided, he would imitate *Ajji*'s mannerisms and her voice, but he was far from anything that could be considered music! He pretended to get carried away by his music, and would wink at *Ajji* and say, 'How's it?' *Ajji* would feign anger, laughing inwardly.

Now, the silence around that boisterous house, after the passing away of so many people, is eerie. A legacy can't just be passed on, there have to be takers for it.

Gaṅgāvataraṇa

I first met Gangubai Hangal in 2005, a few days ahead of her ninety-second birthday, in Hubli. I waited at her residence, the hall of which was the Gangubai Hangal Museum. There were pictures, mementoes, awards and citations all around me. The frail and wrinkled grand old lady, among the few original maestros of the Kirana *gharana*, emerged holding on to her trusted walking stick from behind a flowery, soiled curtain, which quite successfully concealed the yellowing walls and peeling plaster of that part of the house. With a cheery expression, she tucked herself into a wooden chair that had been dusted and stacked with soft cushions to comfort her bony form. "Where are you from? What's your name?" she had asked, bending forward, in typical grandmotherly fashion.

Since that first unforgettable visit, I have lost count of the number of trips I have made to Hubli, and each time she would ask, "Where are you from? What did you say your name was?" I often wondered whether this was something she asked by force of habit, a way of dusting her memory. But her response changed in the coming months. She would narrow her eyes, look up at me and quickly say, "Oh … it's you. I have your address in my diary, don't I?" pulling her faded red diary out of her ladylike, shining black 1970s style handbag. Holding it close to her creased-up eyes, she would hunch over the book, turning each leaf carefully, for some pages hung loose, threatening to fly away. Turning to the page marked D, she would say: "Aa … You live in Bangalore. I will come to your house when I come to see my brother Sheshu, okay?"—and would quickly put the diary back into her handbag and shove it under her pillow, as if she were hiding a priceless treasure. I realized that, for her, the bag, the diary, and some odd bits of paper which came from different periods of her past, were precious. They carried the smell and texture of the bygone years, and were the only tangible keys that led her to those invaluable memories.

"Will someone make tea for her …?" she'd call out feebly in the direction of the kitchen, raising her scrawny hands, moving further up her bed to make place for me beside her. While tea was being set to boil in the loyal aluminium vessel with several dents and shades of black patches to boot, she would drop a pinch of powdered *badi saunf* into my palm from among the many tiny boxes that formed a line on her bedside, end to end. "It keeps the breath fresh and is good for digestion. I always have it," she would say, watching the expression on my face as I put the aromatic *saunf* into my mouth. She would then put some grains into her mouth, making sure her fingers didn't touch her tongue. Her jaw would puff out, as she stuck the tip of her tongue right under the only two teeth left in her upper jaw. Savouring it like some high cuisine, she would click her tongue noisily. Proper that she was, Gangubai would immediately pull out her handkerchief from under the pillow, dab her mouth and look at me.

"I keep everything around me. It's easier that way … Have you seen my mother's music book? It's more than a hundred years old," she moved on. "What lovely handwriting!" she muttered to herself, unwrapping with shaky hands the weathered plastic cover in which she preserved her priceless inheritance. "This *keertane* is in *Sriranjani* raga, right?" she would ask, holding the book in my direction but not letting go of it.

Her family was always welcoming, and during my visits I was fortunate to spend hours with her. She would chat endlessly, being cheerful and fussy by turns. Sometimes we just sat in total silence to the background sounds of the blaring television, a grating mixer, or an everyday, high-pitched family conversation.

In such moments I would try to dig deeper. Gangubai's silence, in fact, interested me more than her speech. Each time I was left with a gnawing feeling that there was much more. Both she and I knew that we had set ourselves afloat in a sea of partial truths. There were moments in her that refused to crystallize into words: they existed only as silences or erasures. There were parts to her story she couldn't explain. Her experiences were intense, but they never sublimated into grand theories of life. I was meeting her on the threshold of ninety-three, and at that age I presume there is baggage one wants to shed. Her silence had only grown sharper with the adding years.

Unlike Begum Akhtar, who was clearly unabashed and could take the world by its horns, and Kesarbai Kerkar, who could be smug and snotty, Gangubai was acquiescent. She was stunningly simple, yet deep. Her conviction to live according to her beliefs was seldom expressed in words.

What was I looking for? People often asked me, "What do you plan to write?" which is exactly the question I posed to myself. In that regard there is a fascinating story about Leo Tolstoy and his novel *Anna Karenina.* A strand of hair lying on a pathway apparently caught the writer's attention. He was so struck by its beauty that he imagined it on the protagonist of the novel he had just finished writing. After this, his work could no longer remain the same. He returned home to rewrite the novel in its entirety!

A single strand of hair demanded a different telling. And here I am, confounded by the multiple strands and the many possibilities that lie before me. In my mind, as I walked that summer morning into "Ganga Lahari", Gangubai's house, she was still a star of the musical firmament. Her full-bodied, masculine voice held sway over generations of listeners, and hadn't spared me either. But the person I met was hardly the diva I had seen on stage. When I started making frequent visits in 2007, I saw some of it in spirit, even though most of its existence lay irretrievably in the past.

Her eyes scrunched up, she was trying hard to read and hum a *keertane* her mother used to sing, keeping beat with her right hand. She was smiling to herself. Pulling herself out of her world when she registered my presence, she looked up towards me and said, "Why do I get a fever every day? Can I take half a Crocin? It troubles me ...." This world hadn't been easy for her to negotiate, especially with people constantly taking stock of her lived life.

A slight change in the emphasis of the musical note evokes a different mood and weaves a different thought and melodic pattern. If life amounts to the variation between allied ragas, Gangubai Hangal's life has been a sure example of it.

Her journey to the sublime is chequered with the loss of love, loss of self, disappointments and anguish. Time plays truant. It douses the past in a romantic haze. In retrospect it fills one with courage. Things become so distant that indulgence takes over. The objective philosophical gaze redeems the past from its traumatic moments. And truth is always considered in retrospect—a recollected emotion. Even if all the details of life and music were laid out then, the mysteries would remain, with their sense of incompleteness.

It is impossible for any serious student of music and history to consider the lives of Gangubai or other extraordinary women isolated from their contexts. Coming from their socially disadvantaged backgrounds, such women showed enormous moral grit and determination in achieving what they did. In the 1920s and 1930s, not many girls in India could have come as far as Gangubai. If Tolstoy did not live and write in the times he did, was not born into his circumstances, he probably wouldn't have written the novels he wrote. The same is true of Gangubai. Despite her individualistic vision of life, she and her art were products of her context.

By seeking refuge in Guru Sawai Gandharva, entering the concert stage, the world of films and playback singing, radio and recording studios, Gangubai, who came from the *devadasi* community, had shut doors on the kind of life her mother and grandmother lived. These self-assured moves of her musical life would, however, contradict her unquestioning submission to her husband and his large extended family.

Gangubai was never a feminist icon, but in her own quiet, non-militant approach, she occupied an important place in the established male bastion of the musical world. Her contemporaries, such as Hirabai Badodekar, Mogubai Kurdikar, Kesarbai Kerkar, Rasoolan Bai, Jaddan Bai, Begum Akhtar and Bangalore Nagarathnamma, turned around their less fortunate circumstances in amazing ways as well, but they have been relegated to the dark corners of history. These women soldiered on with determination and persistence from the margins to centre stage, battling social shackles. In them, one finds a complex mélange of rebellion and acceptance, which extends the bounds of tradition towards an unknown modernity.

Gangubai was often asked why she did not sing Bhakti compositions. For her, the music her guru imparted to her was so spiritual that she found no need to sing devotional music. Every aspect of her life was an act of faith—the music as well as the milling everydayness. Carrying firewood for household needs, feeding a huge family, and going through gruelling music sessions—Gangubai did everything with quiet commitment.

When I met her, she was an old woman coping with a failing body and fading glory. But she continued to be an extension of all that she had been in the past. To find her, I had to enter the complex time zones she manoeuvred. I had to unlearn. The pitcher had to be shattered— as Kabir says. I hoped to rediscover a woman who occupied a niche in contemporary musical folklore. She was a woman caught in the throes of circumstance, who embodied diverse historical forces, and one for whom popular mythology may have been the shell underneath which she protected the intense pangs of her private self.

The past is never dead, it is not even the past

Memories are bridges, but they can be burdens too. Remembering her past, the nonagenarian Gangubai would habitually swing between these two poles of memory. The past seemed to stick on adamantly. When I would sit before her for hours, egging her to talk, she would be as unbending as a rod, only letting out the half-word or half-sentence, holding on to her memories like a stubborn child.

"I can't see a single soul from this room! It is so cut off from the world. At best, I see stray cattle," she grumbled about the changed design of her home, Ganga Lahari, in the quiet Deshpande Nagar, in Hubli. "What's life without seeing people and talking to them …? My old, little house was just fine. I could see the street from my window, and would often strike a conversation with passers-by …" She was clearly unhappy about the recent renovation. And then, changing the topic, she mumbled, "Did Krishna have to go before me? It is a curse to see your children die. Why is my pain unending …?"

I remembered her house from my first visit—that is, before the facelift. Gangubai had resided in a longish rectangular space at the back of the house: her room on the left and the kitchen on the right. It opened into the backyard facing the road. It had pictures of the two iconic Kirana maestros, Ustad Abdul Karim Khan and Sawai Gandharva, a squarish niche in the wall had her daughter Krishna's picture, with a red hibiscus flower from the garden adorning the head of the picture frame. The forehead had a large dot of vermilion paste stuck on it, all dried up with tiny cracks. Bits and pieces from her past—yellow, limp objects—had collected on her bed. Little tatters of cloth with zigzag ends, a miniature pocket calendar with the picture of a *math* seer on the reverse, a weathered newspaper-cutting of the Kannada daily *Samyukta Karnataka*, a Parry's confectionery box from the years when desires hadn't assumed such enormous proportions, an Iodex jar, *badi saunf* powder, some peppermint, a little napkin that could come in handy, a box full of plasters, pieces of paper, and such knick-knacks. Tucking herself right in the middle of this snug assortment of objects, Gangubai had unwound to the days before the facelift, her voice soaking in fulfilment: "This is the room where my guru Sawai Gandharva stayed; now I stay here. When he was ill, I kept him with me and nursed him back to good health. I can feel his presence in the room." A moment later, her voice had dipped. "Krishna, too, spent her last days here … They can do what they want with the rest of the house, but this room cannot be touched; it has to be intact … I've told them …" she had said with finality.

"I wonder how the Shukravarapete house is," she spoke after a long pause. I, too, was wondering about it.

"I'm going there tomorrow," I said, taking my time to come out of the world she had woven for me.

Gangubai, who had till then been curled up, with her feet tucked firmly into her soft cotton sari, her arms wound up in the comfort of the *pallu* which had a subtle spray of tiny pink and yellow flowers, woke up shakily with a rush of enthusiasm, resting her hands on the pillow.

"Are you going there? Do you know how to get there? Ask someone for Kamanakatte, Yeligara Oni … It's close to the Veerabhadra Temple … Are you sure you'll go?"

I nodded in assurance. Bending over the edge of her cot, she reached out to me and thrust her feeble, warm fingers into my hands, expecting me to lock my fists reassuringly.

"Will you come back to tell me if the tulsi *katte* in the front is intact …? There was a black stone there … Nobody knew where that stone came from. We had no clue if it was sacred. So we decided to just leave it there. It was my grandmother's idea to build a tulsi *katte* over it. My mother had a special attachment to it … She would fuss endlessly over the tulsi plant and the *katte* …" she said without pausing for breath, forgetting that she had been angry.

The location is 23, Khondapur Road. A narrow, bumpy *kutcha* lane that looked completely disconnected from the rest of the verdant Dharwad landscape. On the dry and dusty road, I asked passers-by for "Gangubai Hangal's house" and was met with puzzled looks. After a couple of failed exchanges, a good Samaritan clad in a soiled dhoti and a dull white shirt, his mouth stuffed with betel and areca, pointed to a spot further down the road.

I arrived at a modest tea shop opposite an old flour mill. There it was, at the intersection of Lakkammanahalli Oni and Yeligara Oni, a weather-beaten and dilapidated house. A portion of the house had crumbled, anthills hardened with age and tall wild weeds stuck out from all corners of the rundown portion. A strange exhilaration filled me as I encountered this ruin. I went up the two broken steps and stood in front of the door. There was a rusty metal piece fastened to the door's wooden frame. The letters engraved on it had nearly disappeared. Standing on the tip of my toes, I ran my fingers over the grainy metal piece: it said 1909. I had to see Gangubai from here—the little girl who pranced about in the waiting room of history.

This crumbling structure had been a seat of music for passionate musicians of yesteryear, like Abdul Karim Khan, Sawai Gandharva, Mallikarjun Mansur and others, who would stop by to listen to the gifted Carnatic vocalist Ambabai. In fact, for Ustad Abdul Karim Khan, the place was no less than Thanjavur itself—the seat of Carnatic music. Time does not leave physical imprints, but all this was firmly etched in Gangubai's mind.

When I returned that evening, she was running a temperature. Her bones were hurting. She was giving herself a hot pack, while Potamma, her nurse of ten years, dotingly looked on.

"Did you get to see my mother's house?" she asked as soon as she saw me. Extracting every detail out of me, not once but twice over, she made sure she got a complete picture of the house. Her face lit up when I told her that the tulsi *katte* had survived the ravages of time. "Did you see the Veerabhadra Temple? The gramophone shop I practically spent the whole day in was close to it," she recalled.

The young Gangu was fascinated by the shellac records that spun on a stubbed spindle. She habitually immersed herself in the timeless melodies they churned out. Zohrabai Agrewali was her favourite, and there was hardly an occasion when Gangu returned home without her songs.

"My mother was so cultured and sophisticated. She had kept the house and the front yard spic and span," Gangubai said. Ambabai washed the yard with cowdung water, nurtured the tulsi plant and decorated it with flowers, and never missed the rangoli. In the predominantly Brahmin locality, a newcomer often mistook Ambabai's house to be a devout upper-caste household.

"Krishna was like my mother in many ways. Very pious. Every morning, she spent hours in the puja room …" she choked, lying down in exhaustion. This time it's not just physical exhaustion: it's the boulder of memories that weighs her down. Tears run down her cheeks, and she looks for her handkerchief under her pillow.

"Once I complained to my guru that Krishna doesn't practise the *kharaj*. After a pause, he looked towards me and said, 'Her voice texture doesn't require it, Gangu. Yours does.' See—I had not realized—only gurus can tell you these finer aspects. What's life without a guru!"

During the four years of my visit, she had been hospitalized several times—for various ailments, big and small. She always had a flood of visitors—from the security guard's aunt to the ward boy's kid brother to her disciple's uncle's mother-in-law to the chief minister. After the initial "What's your name?", "Where are you from?" she invariably drifted into her own world. "Did you hear that Bhimanna has been given the Bharatha Ratna?"—was followed by a story from the Kundagol days. She repeated the same story endlessly to every visitor, each time she recalled it as if for the first time in years.

"This hospital has no toilet apparently … This bedpan kills me," she would say, taking the visitor completely by surprise. "In those days, when I attended programmes, I was always worried about toilets. There was no problem in the trains though."

Turning to her nurse she had said: "I'm leaving for home early in the morning tomorrow, you can tell the doctor …"

"That's right … Why even tell the doctor, *ajji*?! Is there a doctor better than your own self? Just pick up your bag and walk out, *ajji*," her grandson Manoj Hangal would joke.

"What doctors! In those days, they would feel your pulse and give you medicine. And the patient would be fine in a couple of days. Now, they prick endless holes in my body just to find out what's wrong …!" she would feign anger.

On any given day, a conversation with Gangubai certainly had three people in it: Ambabai, Sawai Gandharva and Krishna. They were windows to her life. Seeing through these, one could glean how intensely her emotions and art were intertwined. She made difficult choices, but to see them in the isolated contexts of gender or art was to diminish her as an object of study. She could never have been an anthropologist's delight; nothing in her was dead material. Her past lived vibrantly in the present. She lived in a world that was quick to fix her in particular ways; however, her expression belied any such attempt, standing as a testimony to the play of time.

In speaking about her life, she also spoke of the many Ambabais and Krishnas, and of extraordinary gurus like Sawai Gandharva whose deep commitment to music helped them soar above their individual selves as well as their contexts. Her life was like a folk song, with a simple exterior holding deep, resounding reverberations within.

Gangubai's memory always moved back and forth, so does mine. To tell her story in chronological order is to take away her living presence in me, to strip it of all its complexities, as well as its simplicity.

There are numerous strings in my lute

No individual has ever begotten all her meanings: several forces shape her in ways tangible and intangible. Gangubai was no exception. In fact, by the time she was born in 1913, the country was already in the middle of a cultural renaissance, a powerful response to the projects of the Empire. Even as she may have been oblivious to the great cultural and political churning of her time, she was nevertheless in the midst of it. A study of Gangubai's life and her music can never be two separate things. Neither of these could escape the forces of the times, and thereby largely determined each other. While it is true she stood to alter the course of history, she was also its product. In the course of narrating her life, she would admit to the influence of her times in her subjective narration of her past. Her state of mind was a reminder of the Buddha's way—a creative withdrawal into the spirit. Throughout her career, she dwelt on and developed the consciousness of the past, living in a continued state of surrender to tradition, that allowed her to extinguish her musical personality in it. If this appears as a leitmotif in the entire narration, it is because Gangubai never spoke without referring to the past masters. If Gangubai Hangal the musician existed, it was only as part of a living tradition.

While trying to present a narrative about her life and music, I had to ask the following questions. How did cultural authorities fashion themselves in her time? How were they drafted into the historical projects of an emerging nation? What was its impact on the musician and on prevailing musical tastes? This slew of questions leads one to understand that neither her life nor her music can be studied in isolation. What does it mean to be a minor character in the flow of history? What kind of a relation does this minor character have to the grand course of history? How did Gangubai, someone who could easily have disappeared into the folds of history, move to a position from where she determined it? Gangubai can be understood only when these questions are addressed.

Edward Said, the great postcolonial theorist, had the following insight is his work *Music at the Limits*:

> The study of music can be more, and not less, interesting if we situate music as taking place, so to speak, in a social and cultural setting .... Think of the affiliation between music and social privilege or between music and nation, or between music and religious veneration—and the idea will be clear enough …

It is in this matrix of interconnectedness that I hope to read Gangubai's musical journey.

Musical traditions have informed India's consciousness for several centuries. Classical and folk traditions have always been in constant conversation. Bigger, classical traditions have drawn from the smaller, non-classical ones. The medium of musical practice has also allowed for successive transformations in equations of caste, class and gender.

Tradition is hardly a mere "handing down", it is not something that flows naturally from mother to daughter or guru to *shishya.* "It cannot be inherited," but is obtained through hard labour. In Gangubai, one sees an individual hewing herself in relation to tradition. One sees simultaneously the timeless and the temporal. Her tremendous devotion to the wisdom of her gurus only allowed for the formation of her singular musical personality in the face of rapid changes taking place during her time.

In the beginning of the twentieth century, Karnataka did not yet boast a history of Hindustani music. The princely state of Mysore had been the seat of Carnatic music and its influence was far and wide. But in the span of the coming hundred years, the birth and growth of Hindustani music in Karnataka and its outstanding contribution to the national music scene seems fictional. How did Karnataka become such a fertile ground for the growth of the nation's finest Hindustani music? Most roads lead to Mysore. If the musical landscape of Karnataka is rich and diverse, the credit goes to the maharajas of Mysore.

Though the two systems of Indian music—Hindustani and Carnatic—have a history of over 2,000 years going right back to the pre-Vedic times, Hindustani music hadn't made its way down south till the late nineteenth century. By then, the tradition of Carnatic music had made deep inroads in these parts, having been nurtured for over seven centuries. In fact, Gangubai's immediate ancestors—her grandmother and great-grandmother—were practitioners of Carnatic music. The most renowned court in the southern parts for musical patronage was that of Mysore. It provided royal patronage to individual musicians, institutions were set up to teach music, and it helped establish connections with European music publishers and record producers. Its concern for musical education made Mysore's court, especially after 1900, significantly different from other courts like Thanjavur. The maharajas of Mysore were visionary: for them, taking forward a tradition also meant reinventing it with time.

Hence, the hundred years between 1850 and 1950, you see four kings passionate about music, taking it forward in the state in distinct ways. Nalvadi Krishnaraja Wodeyar IV laid emphasis on preservation and teaching. He institutionalized music and founded the Royal School of Music at the Mysore Palace. In his time, each court musician was assigned to teach a certain number of students. A big patron of Hindustani classical music, he also encouraged the study of European music. Between 1920 and 1930, the bands of the Mysore Palace produced gramophone recordings which were made available commercially. The palace account books reveals that the most extravagant expenditures were on acquiring pianos, harmoniums, organs, and other rare instruments. Their musicians were paid handsomely too. By the 1930s, Krishnaraja Wodeyar installed microphones in the Durbar Hall with loudspeakers fixed outside the palace. The Durbar Hall, a site of high culture, was thrown open to the public. With this, music was no longer an affair of the privileged. It also marked the beginning of the transformation of traditional listening practices.

It is a curious coincidence that both the entry of Hindustani classical music into Karnataka and the coming of the phonograph to India occurred at about the same time—in the beginning of the twentieth century. In fact, these two occurrences have a direct bearing on each other. If Gangubai chose to be a Hindustani musician, the gramophone had a big role to play in her decision.

It was in 1898 that the Gramophone Company was established in London. The young American pianist Frederick William Gaisberg went on to join the company as its first recording engineer. He came to India in 1901 to set up the record trade in the east. He was looking for talented musicians, and persuading them to perform for the Gramophone Company. However, in course of time, the company grew beyond business interests and, quite unknowingly, had launched into a massive cultural project. This would determine public taste and gradually unify the country musically.

Fifteen years later, the gramophone—with its huge horn, and the rotating plate from which emanated waves and waves of mesmerizing music—cast a spell on little Gangu as well. She would sit before it and stare at the unbelievable gizmo for hours. Once the fascination for this magical contraption had worn out, her attention turned towards the sounds that it was emanating. Little did she know that it was to become a lasting fixation. From the moment she woke up, she would wait to go to Tamhankar's shop and listen to the music he played. "When Tamanna first played Zohrabai Agrewali, I was enchanted, stunned into silence. What a voice! And she could do anything with it. That woman would sing in black three!" Gangubai once recalled, her face melting into a nostalgic, dreamy expression.

It was 14 November 1902, almost a decade before Gangubai was born. A makeshift recording studio was set up in two large rooms of a hotel in Calcutta by the Gramophone Company. Gaisberg, who was in India with his assistants, had launched a massive search for local musicians. A committed officer and himself a musician, he visited several theatres, *baithaks* and *mehfil*s in Calcutta, seeking the help of the local police superintendent. On one of these expeditions, he was greatly enchanted by the fantastic singing talent of a nautch girl, a *tawaif.* Gauhar Jan was her name. She was an Armenian Jew who had taken to Islam, and had been trained in more than one *gharana* of music. The stunningly beautiful lady of phenomenal talent fixed her charges at a whopping Rs 3,000! And surely enough, Gaisberg and his team agreed. At the end of the three-minute recording she stylishly announced in English—"My name is Gauhar Jan."

Gauhar Jan, the queen of *thumri*, became a pioneer. She mastered the technique of making three-minute presentations, something the erstwhile ustads had scoffed at. Between 1902 and 1920 she had cut over sixty records, through which she helped preserve the musical tradition of over three to four generations.

The gramophone had, by then, become hugely popular. Gauhar Jan's haunting voice travelled to several parts of the country, and within no time she had begun to receive performance invitations from various princely states. She became synonymous with the *thumri*s "*Radhe Krishna Bol Mukhase*" and "*Krishna Murari Binat Karat*". They gained such wide favour that many singers began to sing them at their concerts. Speaking of her earliest memory of the gramophone, Gangubai mentioned Gauhar Jan's "*Radhe Krishna Bol Mukhase*", which she pointed out was also a favourite of Hirabai Badodekar. Legend has it that Gauhar Jan, too, was a great admirer of Hirabai—the daughter of the founder of the Kirana *gharana,* Abdul Karim Khan—and had apparently taught the latter a number of bhajans and *thumri*s from her rich repertoire. Both Hirabai and Sunderabai duly recorded these on gramophone records. From all the written material on the life and times of Gauhar Jan, and other histories of the time that refer to her, it is evident that not many were able to escape the charm of her music.

It did not take long for Gauhar Jan's fame to reach the south. Speaking of her performance in Bangalore on 20 April 1912 at the Bowring Institute, H.P. Krishna Rao, editor of *The Indian Music Journal*, observed: "She possesses a sweet voice which when prolonged seems uniformly grand, more so, as it is produced without any strain." In fact, Pt. Vishnu Narayan Bhatkhande, the pioneering musicologist, would often say that she was one of the greatest woman singers of India.

Gauhar Jan had also succeeded in captivating the royalty of Mysore. Irrespective of the genre of music, the best musicians were customarily brought to the Mysore Palace for a performance. Krishnaraja Wodeyar was so mesmerized by her music that he invited her to his court and honoured her. Much later, in 1928, Gauhar Jan did join the service of the Mysore state on a salary of Rs 500, an unthinkable figure even for those holding the highest offices in the state machinery of that time. She died in 1930, after having served the court for barely eighteen months.

The gramophone had no doubt stormed the country, popularizing Hindustani classical music in leaps and bounds. The Mysore kings, however, looked beyond the gramophone as well. They were serious about promoting established maestros. Ghulam Abbas Khan, who was Ustad Faiyaz Khan's grandfather, was a favourite of the Mysore king. Having heard the Agra *gharana* doyen Nathan Khan in Bombay and being struck by his music, the maharaja appointed him as court musician of Mysore. After Nathan Khan's death in 1901, he appointed Ustad Vilayat Hussain Khan in his place. Nathan Khan's son Abdullah Khan, Barkatullah Khan, Abdul Karim Khan saab, Abdul Wahid Khan, Bhaskarbua Bakhle, Neelkanthbua Mirajkar, Kesarbai Kerkar and several others were honoured and patronized by the kings of Mysore. Records show that the Hindustani classical musicians were paid much higher than their Carnatic musicians.

The Mysore Palace was democratic in its cultural outlook, facilitating fascinating exchanges between Carnatic and Hindustani music. It was only because of the maharajas that the two styles coexisted in these parts, in contrast to the insular life of Hindustani music in most of north India. The court musicians were given a free hand in bringing the best musical minds to the court of

Mysore. Kumar Prasad Mukherji tells an interesting story in an anecdotal essay on the Kirana *gharana* in his work *The Lost World of Hindustani Music*. Abdul Karim Khan, who was later hailed as the pioneer of the Kirana style, gave a performance in Meerut along with his brother Latif. It was the late nineteenth century, and he was only eleven years old then. The duo sang such an exquisite Multani that the audience begged for an encore. This was followed by an excellent *Poorvi*, and Hyder Baksh, the sarangi player at the court of Mysore, who was present at the concert, was so impressed by the performance that he showered his blessings on them. He had turned to Ustad Kale Khan and said, "You must bring these lads to Mysore for the Dussera celebrations and I will present them to the maharaja."

Six years later, as Mukherji notes in the essay, Abdul Karim Khan arrived at the court of Mysore during the rule of Krishnaraja Wodeyar IV, and gave an enchanting performance. The royalty showered him with shawls and gold coins. This was the beginning of a lasting relationship that Khan saab had with Mysore, and in fact the whole of Karnataka.

When introduced to the grandeur of Carnatic music, Khan saab was ecstatic. Mukherji puts it on record:

> The Carnatic musicians were much taken in by the high, melodious voice of Abdul Karim just as he found the preponderance of sargams in Carnatic music highly intriguing. No doubt his simple, but beautiful sargams, which we find in his later 78-rpm records, owed their origin to this momentous occasion. The only other Hindustani musician one can readily think of who was influenced by Carnatic sargams—and virtually started a new style of singing—was Ustad Aman Ali Khan of Bhindibazar, Bombay.

How did North Karnataka become the centre for Hindustani music? Most musicians who came to the Mysore Palace had to pass through Hubli–Dharwad to reach their destinations in the north. Hubli–Dharwad–Kundagol–Belgaum invariably became their halt points on their way back. For many of them, these places did not remain mere stopovers, they gradually began to develop an emotional bond with the place and its music-loving public.

This was true especially of Ustad Abdul Karim Khan. The process that began in Mysore eventually established itself firmly in North Karnataka. So much so that, after the Unification, it seemed that South Karnataka always had affiliations to Carnatic music, whereas North Karnataka had to Hindustani.

Abdul Karim Khan travelled so often to Mysore that both on his onward journey and return he made stops at Hubli and Dharwad, sang for small, private gatherings, and was greatly enthusiastic about listening to the local musicians. It was during one of these visits that he had stumbled upon the music of Ambabai, who belonged to a family of professional singers. Listening to her was a spiritual experience for the Ustad, and he never passed Dharwad without stopping at her residence. Ambabai's music gave him the feeling that he was in Thanjavur. Abdul Karim Khan—like many other musicians of his time—was so unabashed about his love for Carnatic music, that he did not consider it blasphemous to sing *Devagandhari* and *Ananda Bhairavi* for 78 rpms. The *Anand Bhairavi* that he expounded was actually the *Bhairavi* of the Carnatic style. If Ambabai in Dharwad cast a major influence on him, so did the legendary Veena Dhanammal, who had a highly individual perception of music. When Ariyakudi Ramanuja Iyengar's kutcheri format was making a sensation in the Madras concert scene, and musicians were taking to it like bees to honey, Dhanammal held on to her beliefs firmly.

Khan saab stayed in Dhanammal's house each time he went to Madras. He was even forced to change his opinion about *kalpanaswaras* after listening to her extraordinary music. As a tribute to these women of rare artistry—Ambabai, Dhanammal and others—Khan saab recorded the *Kharaharapriya kriti* "*Rama Nee Samanamevaru*" and the *Saveri* composition "*Entha Nerchina*". His renditions may not have gained the approval of the masters of Carnatic music, but they were outstanding gestures to a great tradition. Their importance was heightened because they came from a Hindustani musician of his stature and calibre. The intellectual indebtedness these performers were capable of expressing is indeed astounding. It is important to note that these very moments reshaped the expression of the Kirana tradition. The legendary performers who belonged to this style were, even later, constantly assimilating to it and synthesizing it in many different ways to carve the Kirana note.

The history of performing pasts is so fluid that its beginnings cannot be fixed at exact chronological points, or narrowed down to definite influences. Due to its continuous evolution, the more you try to locate the beginning, the deeper you move into the past. Hence, any effort to locate the exact point at which the Hindustani classical music tradition came to establish itself in the Hubli–Dharwad region is like riding a pendulum.

The musician who went on to become the torchbearer of the Kirana tradition—the man who served as the most crucial link between Karim Khan saab and the later legends of Kirana who fired the melodic imagination of this country—met Abdul Karim Khan saab in the most ordinary of circumstances. Yet, this commonplace meeting was charged with the power of myth. Khan saab was staying at Kundagol, where he met the eager beaver music enthusiast Rambhau Kundagolkar, who constantly hovered around the maestro, desperate for a single glance from him. In the years to come, the man—the inimitable Sawai Gandharva—would go on to become the leading light of the Kirana *gharana.* The other direct disciple of Karim Khan saab was Ganpatrao Gurav, who was a court musician at Jamkhandi. In this manner, the Kirana *gharana* took firm roots in Karnataka. Yet another musician from the north, the maestro of Gwalior Bhaskarbua Bakhle—who was at consummate ease with the Agra and Jaipur *gharanas*—visited these parts frequently.

If winds of Hindustani music blew over North Karnataka from the heart of Mysore Presidency, the Bombay Presidency brought its influence as well—especially through the modern sensibility of the Marathi stage. According to the late cultural historian Ashok D. Ranade in his book *The Stage Music of Maharashtra,* this rising "modern sensibility" was a cumulative effect of two tendencies: an innate desire to project Indian identity as a cultural response to the colonial powers, and at the same time, quite contrarily, an outer assimilation of the inspiring elements of occidental culture.

Annasaheb Kirloskar, a key innovator in the Marathi sangeet-natak tradition, was born in Gurlhosur, Karnataka. For the most part, he grew up in Dharwad, and took up a government job in Belgaum. He founded the theatre company Kirloskar Natak Mandali. He was well acquainted with the musical tradition of Karnataka, and travelled widely with his plays. He had watched actor-singers taking part in *Sangeeta-Parijataka* and other plays. With singers like Balkoba Natekar and Moroba Wagholikar in his company, Annasaheb also tried to include attractive melodies from the Carnatic style in his work. The entry of the legendary actor-musician Bal Gandharva took the Kirloskar Natak Mandali to new heights. The rich tradition of the Haridasi *kirtan** style of singing also made an important contribution to stage music in Maharashtra.

There can be many histories of music, each with its own perspective. While some interpret the history of twentieth-century Indian music as a movement from conservative tradition to liberal modernity, others see it as a shift from intellectual and classical modes to popular style. In any given period, however, music could only be understood as a cumulative effect, as the sum total of ongoing changes in the fabric of social, political and cultural life.

Gangubai Hangal was born into a time when the musical scene in India was charged with intellectual activity and passionate emotional energy. New forms of communication—particularly recording and preserving—had not only transformed the reception of music, but had also broadened horizons of understanding. Her music held many polarities in tension—tradition and innovation, system and originality, the personal and impersonal. The past was such a living presence in her, that her music had a complex inclusiveness. It was never dull and academic.

---

* While the "*kirtan*" is a north Indian usage for a musical composition in the light musical genre—mostly bhajans, abhangs, etc., the "*keertane*" is a term used in Carnatic classical music for a standardized composition by a *vaggeyakara.*

If history is accumulation and development, consolidation and growth, what does a society preserve and nurture? What does it reject and discard? How does it reconstruct the past? How do we in the present set the limits for self and subjectivity? The big picture is important; it must lead to the smaller details. Answers to these questions can be discerned from an examination of the twin worlds that Gangubai straddled as performer and human being.

Marathi *natyasangeet*, at that moment, was looking for an idiom entirely its own: it borrowed elements from *khayal* music, but also absorbed, as in the case of Annasaheb's contribution, elements of Carnatic music as well. It processed these diverse musical elements to produce a distinct Marathi signature, a style that was indigenous to the state—the unmistakable Maharashtrian "lalithya," lilting combination of melodic presentation, intonation and musical graces.

Most major theatre companies beginning from Kirloskar's time (1880) employed classical musicians of high calibre. These musicians were rushed into companies irrespective of their acting capabilities. Pt. Sawai Gandharva, Pt. Vinayakrao Patwardhan, Pt. Mallikarjun Mansur, Pt. Arjun Sa Nakod, Pt. Bhimsen Joshi, Hirabai Badodekar and many others were inducted into roles chiefly because of their singing abilities. There are abundant examples of *natyasangeet* based on traditional *bandish*es. The early plays had fifty to sixty songs in them, and the audience would respond with wild glee listening to them. They hungered for more and pleaded for encores. It wouldn't be far-fetched to say that it was the love for music in fact that took them to theatre. One can only imagine the spirit of the performance when legends like Ustad Ahmedjan Thirakwa played for Bal Gandharva's Gandharva Natak Mandali!

The impact of these *natak mandali*s was so high that very soon Jodhpur, Agra, Meerut, Lahore, Mysore and Gadag saw the birth of theatre groups. Music and theatre, both strongly intertwined, carried in them strong nationalistic aspirations and characteristic regional flavours. Most musicians of Karnataka, like the iconic Mallikarjun Mansur of the Jaipur-Atrauli *gharana*, also began his musical career in theatre. The gramophone industry in India could hardly overlook the popularity of these *natak mandali*s and, by 1920, a whole lot of recordings had been made. More than 113 songs of Bal Gandharva alone had been recorded. The itinerant companies and gramophone recordings left their marks on various geographical corners.

The other important factor that allowed for Hindustani music to have strong roots in North Karnataka, which never had the benefit of royal patronage, was the role the Lingayat *math*s played. In the latter half of the nineteenth century, many of these *math*s became learning centres of Hindustani music. In fact, some of the *math*-heads were themselves practitioners. This can be gathered from the memoirs of people who lived in these parts during that period. In his memoir, Mallikarjun Mansur constantly speaks of his spiritual guru, Shree Mrityunjaya Swami, who was a competent musician himself. He expresses his indebtedness to him through a long verse that sings his praise. We also have stories of how Abdul Karim Khan saab never left Hubli–Dharwad without visiting the Siddharoodha Math. Upon each visit he sang there for a couple of hours.

Most legendary classical musicians from this period were known to have had adventurous and rather eclectic pasts. While some used theatre as a springboard to launch their careers as independent musicians, there were others who, against the wish of their teachers, sang for plays. Mallikarjun Mansur, for the love of music, left home and joined Vamanrao Master's Vishwagunadarsha Theatre Company. In this company, Marol Ramanna and his younger brother Neelakantappa, who were trained by the legendary Master Deenanath Mangeshkar (Lata Mangeshkar's father), doyen of Marathi theatre, formed the musical force. On one occasion, when the company reached Bagalkot, Mansur met Pt. Neelkanthbua Mirajkar, who was immensely impressed by the young Mansur's singing. Neelkanthbua, who was from Bijapur in North Karnataka, became the student of Balkrishnabua Ichalkaranjikar, and was the *gurubandhu* of Vishnu Digambar Paluskar. After seeking rigorous training under him, Mansur returned to Dharwad at the age of sixteen. In 1928, he went back to the Company. Basavaraj Rajguru,

Basavaraj Mansur, Neelkanth Gadgoli and Venkatrao Ramdurg (both disciples of Sawai Gandharva), Arjuna Sa Nakod and many others had similar trajectories. Their bond with theatre was very strong. But with the demand for musical dramas waning, many of these artistes became full-fledged concert artistes. The stage was, however, their training ground. In a rather indirect way, Gangubai was quite central to these serious and vibrant exchanges between theatre and music. All her fellow musicians, like Mansur, Rajguru, Bhimsen Joshi and Arjun Sa Nakod, were an active part of theatre, including her own guru. Though she never sang for a play, she did sing some *natyasangeet* in her very first recording. This was probably just the limitation of her gender and, besides, she had no personal urge for the life of theatre. The only woman *khayal* musician who had an active theatre life was Hirabai Badodekar—she had her own theatre company and sang for it.

In 1968, a photograph of Gauhar Jan was unveiled in the Deodhar's School of Indian Music in Bombay. Among the eminent musicians, critics and officialdom present on the occasion, musicologist Vamanrao Deshpande was one. He records how Gauhar Jan's music inspired Pt. Govindrao Tembe, the architect of Marathi *natyasangeet,* to introduce "Purab Ang" *thumri* and the *dadra* style into *natyasangeet.* These became creative additions, received wide acclaim and became extremely popular. The songs of *Manapaman* (1911), like "*Prema Seva Sharan*" and "*Chandrika Hi Janu*", heralded a new phase in Marathi theatre music and, to this day, those songs are testimony to the highly evolved musical sensibilities of Tembe, whom Bal Gandharva considered his guru. In such multifarious ways, the early twentieth century proved to be a period of great synthesis in the realm of Indian music. The creative impulses of the great maestros flowed in from several quarters.

The cultural revival in India became much sharper after the defeat in the First War of Indian Independence—the Great Rebellion of 1857. Defeated, humiliated and hurt, the country fell back on its rich reservoirs of vitality. The country was going through an inner transformation, a quiet churning, and this came bursting out in every aspect of human production—science, art, music, literature and politics. Every corner of the country throbbed with an ache for cultural resurgence, and this became an essential part of the nation-building project.

By 1890, the great musicologist Pt. Bhatkhande was contemplating a big revolution in the field of music. He wanted to systematize musical theory and practice: something that had been discussed in the ancient texts, but forgotten by the later practitioners of music (much of it is attributed to their inability to read Sanskrit). He started travelling the length and breadth of the country. He spent enormous amounts of time with ustads of various *gharana*s, collected traditional *bandish*es from them, and ascribed them to notation. It is believed that it was largely his single-handed effort that recorded this music for our national culture and education.

During Bhatkhande's time, in the mid-nineteenth century, music was kept alive by a handful of musicians. They were under the feudal patronage of rajas, nawabs and princes, who treated these musicians as personal property, as a result of which the musicians were confined to their territories and seldom moved beyond the protective gaze of their rulers. This isolation was harmful; they were unexposed to other styles of music, which curbed the natural evolution of their own practice. But, conversely, it led them to practise and perfect their own art in great detail and, therefore, their music became highly individualistic. These individual styles eventually assumed the status of a *gharana.* When Bhatkhande set out on his expedition, there were five to six *gharana*s that dominated the musical map in India.

To release music from the stranglehold of elite patrons, Bhatkhande at this juncture organized over five music conferences and got nationalists and patrons involved in it. In fact, he received appreciation from people like Rabindranath Tagore for his pioneering efforts. Music in India was now moving out of the private realms of the patron, and was taking shape in the public sphere. The most crucial aspect of this shift was that Bhatkhande was consciously seeking to erase the gulf between the patron and the performer, and with the music conferences, the categories of both the performer and the listener (patron) had come to occupy the same social space. Gradually, through Bhatkhande's efforts, an art that was in the hands of the national and state elite became the public culture of India. In the years that followed, within the next two decades or so, Gangubai had managed to make such strides for herself. As the music of the nation moved out of the patron's threshold, Gangubai also changed things for the *devadasi*s. Resolutely and quietly, she was leaving behind an unpleasant social past.

She came from a family of robust women—women who stood bravely in the face of adversity and hardship. Gangubai's moral fabric was largely shaped by these women of enormous courage and conviction. However, it would perhaps be unfair to singularly attribute her grit to just the women of her family. Her spirit was also being shaped by the exemplary women of her times, unconsciously.

In the mid-nineteenth century, the British usurped more Indian kingdoms, bringing these territories under their control. This imperial project of expansion did not take place without violence and bloodshed. The British, with all their might, tried to crush local rulers and lords. The small-time rulers retaliated valiantly to the more powerful enemy. Some of the sparks of the 1857 uprising had reached the Bombay Presidency as well. In the years 1857-58, the kings of Surapura, Naragunda, Dharwad and Halagali revolted against the British.

Gangubai's great-grandmother Gangavva was patronized by the chief accountant of Babasaheb, a very powerful Brahmin ruler of Naragunda. When the revolt intensified, the kings of the neighbouring provinces of Hemmige, Dambala, Soratur and Goa joined hands with Babasaheb in fighting the British, who had in turn stepped up their battle. The British army, led by their chieftain Meesan, was all set to capture Babasaheb and Bhimrao Mundargi of Dharwad. However, the enemy got the better of the British. Meesan had pitched his tents at Sureban, close to Ramdurg. One morning they were taken by total surprise. Babasaheb and his men attacked the British army. Meesan was killed in 1858.

What followed was an act of venegeance. The angry British turned up with a huge army and gheraoed the Naragunda fort. Babasaheb's men fled. Some fell into the hands of the British as well. The British cornered Gangavva, hoping to extract information out of her. They felt Gangavva was the sure route to Babasaheb. They taunted, harassed and traumatized her. But nothing would weaken her will. She wouldn't breathe a word about Babasaheb's whereabouts even when swords were hanging menacingly above her head. Gangavva, extremely courageous and intelligent, looked for the right moment and made an escape from the clutches of the British. The brave woman mounted a horse and rode fearlessly until she reached Hangal. By this unexpected turn of circumstances, Gangavva eventually came to settle down in Hangal and made it her home. The British failed to trace her. But soon, they did track down Babasaheb in Naragunda, and without further delay sentenced him to death.

Gangavva, like most women of her community, was proficient in music. She gave birth to a daughter Kamalabai, and toiled hard to raise her. Gangavva recognized her daughter's talent for music and put her through formal training in Carnatic music. In a couple of years, Kamalabai blossomed into a lovely musician and became a sought-after artiste in and around Hangal. She was a devout woman with remarkably sharp musical instincts. Apart from this, not much is known about Kamalabai's life. Whenever Kamalabai's life came up for discussion, Gangubai didn't seem to have too many details. When and why did she move to Dharwad? Gangubai didn't have answers. It's rather surprising that Kamalabai, who outlived her daughter Ambabai and lived her last years with Gangubai, never felt the need to tell her story.

Kamalabai gave birth to a daughter, whom she called Ambabai. The girl, like her mother, was phenomenally talented. Soft-spoken and pious, Ambabai's perseverance was academic. She came to be an outstanding Carnatic musician, far more gifted than her mother, and was in no way inferior to those who had made a name for themselves in the heartland of Carnatic music, the Madras Presidency. Living away from the hub of Carnatic music and with very limited patronage coming her way, Ambabai's music was confined to Dharwad and its surroundings. Even then, the revered Hindustani musicians who made a stop at Dharwad never left without paying a visit to her. In fact, each time Ustad Abdul Karim Khan attended a *baithak* at Ambabai's house, he never failed to say that he felt as if he had visited the abode of Saint Tyagaraja himself! Gangubai's first meeting with the founder of the Kirana *gharana* was when he came to listen to her mother.

These stories lie scattered in obscure nooks and corners. Details of their life and artistry have been pushed into oblivion. The remains are fragmented and disjointed. You can still trace the story, but the gaps are yawning. It is said that when Ambabai sang, her modest house would be teeming with listeners, and they flowed on to the pavement as well. They stood at the window, peered over each other's heads, and elbowed one another to listen to her. One cannot reduce this anticipation to petty curiosity in order to catch a glimpse of the *gaanewaali*, Ambabai's music was much more—it was chaste, austere and sincere. Else, why would it bring ustads like Abdul Karim Khan to her doorstep? But sadly, when Karim Khan saab and Sawai Gandharva sang at the homes of many other upper-caste patrons, Ambabai was denied entry. The woman, who was otherwise revered as a *vidushi,* had to stand by the roadside and listen to the masters.

Gangubai was born in Dharwad on 5 March 1913. How could she possibly escape music?—it was something that she was born into, not only in her home but also in the world beyond her home. Little Gangu, in her long skirt and blouse and two tightly oiled plaits, would scamper on the homely streets of Shukravarapete that would be reverberating with music. The revolutionary gramophone dotted every street, with every teashop proudly displaying its shining, new acquisition. Hardly a few steps from her home, the harmonium-repair shop of Shreepadappa Tamhankar held great attraction for the young Gangu. For her, it was almost like a pilgrim centre. The gramophone industry had been around for a little over a decade. Some reigning musicians had already been recorded by the gramophone companies. When Gaisberg stepped on Indian soil, little did he know what he was doing. Music worked magic in the lives of people far and near, giving birth to many an artiste. He had initiated a quiet revolution in the lives of women who were confined to their homes. They could now pursue their passion without being subject to the male gaze—it was an artistic rebirth for them.

Zohrabai Agrewali was an influential late-nineteenth-century singer. She was a contemporary of Gauhar Jan, during the dying phase of the courtesan-singing tradition in Indian classical music. Despite the obdurate male order, Ustad Faiyaz Khan and Ustad Bade Ghulam Ali Khan had to admit that Zohrabai was an unparalleled musician. The two musicians have even admitted that she was a very inspiring force in their own music. On listening to the no-holds-barred singing of Zohrabai from the very few surviving rpms, one can only surmise the impact it might have had on the little Gangu. Her "*Allah Jane*" in Miya Ki Todi is a two-minute rendition, replete with the fluidity and magnetism of her full-bodied voice. Her improvisations sparkle with imagination. "*Aan-baan jiya ...*" Gangubai had hummed in her shaky, gravelly voice, as she revisited her childhood. It was at Tamhankar's shop that she had first heard her favourite "*Radhe Krishna Bol Mukhase*", a *thumri* that Gauhar Jan had popularized and that Hirabai would also sing.

Most tea stalls had gramophone players. Men with endless cups of hot tea listening to the music spooling out from the enigmatic gadget was a common sight. Women stood at windows or at the doorsteps of their homes on muddy streets, hoping that the wind would blow in their direction and shower them with some exquisite music too. For Gangu, it was sheer joy to run from one tea stall to the other. She would invariably plead with the shopkeepers to play Zohrabai's record. "What will you sing for us if we play the record for you?" they would fondly ask this little enthusiast. Gangu had learnt a few songs from her mother and she would instantly offer to sing for them. The shopkeepers were only too happy to oblige the endearing Gangu.

Between home and the world, Gangubai's life had a lot of music, but it was not necessarily filled with joy. She had more than her share of difficulties, but, always, music was an escape, a solace. Much later in her life, Gangubai did beg to differ. Music was never an escape, she said. But even with her denial, it certainly was a springboard to higher realms.

She did not go to school till she was seven. It did not occur to Ambabai that it was time for the little one to be at school. When she did join, she stopped going after a few days. "Akkavru (teacher) beat my friend," she told her mother and refused to step out. Promptly at school time, she would curl up in a corner, and no one in the world could convince her to go. It was an every-morning ritual, Ambabai would plead with her and Gangu would doughtily refuse. A week passed. One day, the schoolmaster turned up at their house. "What happened to Gangu? Why isn't she coming to school?" he asked Ambabai. Gangubai hid behind her mother and went under her *pallu*. She just wouldn't talk. Finally, Ambabai explained the reason for her absence. "No Gangu, I promise that nobody will beat you … Please come to school, darling … *baaravva* ..." the master, with great patience, convinced her. He was so kind and gentle that Gangu, who was adamant till then, meekly held his hand and walked to school.

The Rashtreeya Vidyalaya was just a furlong away from the house. The school had a huge backyard, where Gangu and her friends played happily before and after classes. "What's that game in which you say 'hu tu tutu' …?"—with a giggle, she recalled her *kabaddi* days. She and her friends had played kabbadi in the backyard so that no one would raise the objection that it was a boys' game. They would play "kho-kho" and "tug of war" as well. "Even with all the difficulties we lived through, what carefree days they were!" she would reminisce. "They wouldn't give us homework. We only had to fill the copy book, that's all."

Her memories of school days also included a conference of the Indian National Congress in Belgaum. She had been taken to Belgaum to sing the welcome-song before the programme. The air was thick with patriotic fervour there, especially with Gandhiji chairing the Congress, and the children's feet wouldn't rest on the ground. She had arrived two days prior to the programme, and a teacher from Mysore taught them the welcome-song. "He taught us *'Swagaatavu swaagatavu sakala jana sankulake*'. But he would pronounce 'sankulake' as 'sammkulake', and this was enough to make me laugh uncontrollably. I got shouted at for it. But tell me, that's not the way to pronounce it, no …?" she would ask mischievously, curling up her lips.

The *pandal* was huge, the stage mammoth. Belgaum was hosting thousands, not just from Karnataka, but from all over the country. All the dignitaries had arrived, and Gandhiji's presence had created magic. "I was so thrilled to see Gandhiji. When they asked us to go up the stage for our song, each one of us wanted to do her best and somehow catch Gandhiji's attention," Gangubai remembered. After the song was over, all the kids who sang had been lined up next to the stage. Gandhiji walked past, smiling at each one of them, and as a matter of pure chance, patted little Gangu on her back. She was elated. "I was too young to listen to speeches. So soon after we finished singing, we were busy chattering away. But when the Mahatma spoke we listened to him with rapt attention."

Lunch had been organized at the *pandal* for the gathering at the conference. People sat down in rows, young and old alike. But nobody had noticed the little Gangu standing quietly in a corner, shying away from the group that had proceeded to lunch. Gopal Rao Deshpande's keen eyes spotted Gangu. This freedom fighter known for his progressive views was the lunch supervisor. The caring, warm gentleman was on his rounds to check if everyone was comfortable, and had found a place to lunch. On seeing Gangu standing alone, he walked towards her. Noticing this from the corner of her eye, she tucked her head into her chest. "Why child, don't you want to eat?" he had asked, lifting her face. Gangu was on the verge of tears, and could hardly speak. When she was finally coaxed into speaking, with tears running down her cheeks, she had said: "First of all they will make me sit separately, since I'm of a lower caste. Then I will have to stay back and do the *goma* (clean up the place after lunch) … So I'd rather be hungry." "*Enankondiyavva* (What do you think, my dear child)? This is Gandhiji's durbar, all are equal here, there is no high and low. Come, I will sit with you ..." he held Gangu's hand reassuringly and made sure she sat beside him for lunch.

"It was for the same reason that my mother would refuse to eat in any Brahmin's house." Ambabai got copious invitations for functions and pujas. They would want her to come and sing for every auspicious occasion. But when it was time for lunch, it was a different story. They would make her sit at a distance, wait till everyone ate, clean up the place, and then eat. "It was traumatic ..." Gangubai would remember.

* * *

If Gangu wasn't at school, she was at Tamanna's shop. And Tamanna, wildly passionate about music himself, would enthusiastically play these plates any number of times for all those who had gathered at his humble shop. Gangu would run back home and promptly sing for her mother all that she had got to hear. And she sang the pieces rather well. Tamanna was himself excited by the manner in which the gramophone had infused their lives with so much music, and would often turn up at Ambabai's house with his leg harmonium. Gangu would sing and Tamanna would accompany her on the harmonium. Years ago in an interview, she related to me how every tea stall and *paan* shop would play gramophone records of classical music in her time, and even the ignorant shepherds would hum *bandish*es and *thumri*s sung by great artistes like Abdul Karim Khan, Hirabai, Narayanrao Vyas, Sunderabai and others.

The gramophone was a major force in the life of both the common man and the musician. For women, it was a boon. The late D.K. Pattamal paid a tribute to the gramophone in a speech she made at the Madras Music Academy in 1970. "In the absence of a family connection to music, my success was due to the gramophone. As a Brahmin girl, I couldn't learn in the traditional *gurukula* method, which would mean living with a male, non-Brahmin teacher. To compensate for this misfortune of not being able to learn music systematically, I learnt from various teachers and listened to gramophone records." In the same speech, Pattamal had also mentioned how the gramophone had enabled her to perform without having to make a public appearance (which was taboo for women from conservative Brahmin homes). It provided her an opportunity to sing without being seen.

Ambabai had been trained under Imamsaheb Harappanahalli and Shamachar of Ranebennur. She was an authority on *padam*s and *javali*s—the choicest repertoire of professional singers in those days, especially because many of these remarkably lyrical compositions were rich in *shringara rasa*, and abounding in erotic suggestion. Whenever Gangubai spoke of her mother, she swelled with pride. She would describe her mother's keen sense of language, which helped her get under the skin of the text of a composition and render it with richness. This unusual ability to interpret invariably heightened the listener's experience. For instance, one of the *javali*s had the words *jade pettige.* Ambabai wouldn't stop at describing the box containing ornaments for the braid. She would first sing it as a statement exploring its literary meaning, then move on to pun on the word *pettige.* She further extended the musical exploration to develop tender, romantic moments in which the "beloved" lovingly raps (*pettu*, as in "a gentle blow") her lover with her braid (*jade*).

Her intelligence brought her many connoisseurs. Krishnarao Gore of Marathi theatre often came to Ambabai to borrow tunes from her rich repertoire. Abdul Karim Khan saab, who spoke a smattering of Kannada and Hindi, would learn songs from her on each of his visits. There were also visitors who wanted her to explain the nuances of the lyric to them. Ambabai had a fairly good collection of books, keeping in mind the little that was available on music in her time. She also had many instruments like the tabla, harmonium and sarangi at home. Deshpande and Shivalingappa, who were music lovers and musicians, often came to her house and spent hours reading the books and consulting her on various musical concepts. Often, they sang before her and were eager for her advice. A Muslim tabla player used to frequent their house. He was from Harappanahalli. Gangubai couldn't recall his name, but remembered that Ambabai took tabla lessons from him. Each class would last a few hours and Ambabai often persuaded him to have food before he left. Little Gangu rolled out betel leaves for him, and he would invariably protest, "I am a Muslim, don't do this for me …" But Ambabai would intervene and say, "You are my guru, and the guru is above religion and caste. You must allow us to serve you." This would silence him.

The house was not sprawling: it was modest but sparkling clean. On entering the house, people big and small would often speak of how it resounded with music, devotion and simplicity. When they passed through Dharwad, artistes like Sunderabai and Hirabai Badodekar would have a *jalsa* at Ambabai's house. In the early years of the twentieth century, Hirabai used to run a theatre company. Her brother Suresh Babu, Sawai Gandharva and Hirabai herself—all the three trained by Abdul Karim Khan saab—were the lead singers of the group. Hence, whenever they camped at Hubli and Dharwad, people thronged to their shows. This was how Hirabai and Ambabai came to know each other and in later years became good friends. Hirabai would stay with Ambabai for eight to ten days, enjoying every bit of her hospitality. Their relationship continued for as long as Ambabai lived, and, after her death, Gangubai nurtured these bonds with care and warmth. Hirabai would continue to come to Hubli and stay at Gangubai's house. Once, even Jaddan Bai, Nargis's mother, performed at their house. This was when Jaddan Bai was a name to reckon with in the field of music and had music directors crying for her attention.

Ambabai's routine every morning began with her practice. This would be followed by lessons for Gangu. "I was being trained by my mother in Carnatic music. Being young, I hadn't made much progress. All I knew was a couple of *keertane*s. In school, I had learnt a couple of Purandaradasa's songs," Gangu remembers. But the gramophone had gradually revealed to Ambabai Gangubai's inclination for Hindustani classical music. This had set her thinking. She had assumed that Gangubai would learn Carnatic music, and that she could train her. But now Ambabai had to find a teacher who could teach the little girl Hindustani music. As her mind was getting prepared for this major shift, Ambabai realized that the time for her to make a big sacrifice was nearing. How could two diverse streams of music co-exist under the same roof?

It was not as if their life, shielded by music, was heavenly and tranquil. Music gave them the strength to face the cruel world. Life at Shukravarapete in Dharwad was hardly a bed of roses for the mother and daughter. It was not a place of happy memories, but one that was crucial in shaping Gangubai's dreams.

Shukravarapete was predominantly a Brahmin locality and the lower castes usually didn't find a place here. If they did, they were hardly given any respect. Kamalabai's family belonged to the Gangamath (ferrymen) caste, and what made it worse was the fact that they were professional musicians. When Gangubai was a little girl, she hardly knew what all this meant. Like any other child of her age, she was playful and mischievous. But what eventually came her way was a harsh blow: something she could never forget all her life. The shock had gained sharpness in retrospect.

"I was five perhaps … In Malmuddi, there were plenty of guava and mango trees I was tempted by. I would approach the trees quietly, and pick the fruits on a sly. Sometimes the neighbours would spot me and scream, 'Why does this daughter of a singer come here? She needs to be thrown out! Who's there …? Throw her out!' I would run back home weeping … Some incidents just stick to you like glue," she would sadly remember. These early bitter experiences had wounded Gangu's natural instinctive self and the minute she stepped on to the street, she would lower her head and walk, as if she had done something that she needed to be ashamed of. The vile street urchins would wait for her to step out. They splashed gutter water on her, and screamed with loathsome pleasure, "*Gaanewaali, gaanewaali.*"

Ironically, the very same evil Shukravarapete neighbourhood had enormous regard for Ambabai's musicianship. No auspicious occasion in the locality was complete without her rendition of Purandaradasa's devotional songs. Ambabai, addressed as

Ambakka, sang for them ungrudgingly. She was quite an authority on Sanskrit and could flawlessly recite Sanskrit shlokas and even explain their meaning. This had silenced the wicked upper-caste neighbourhood to some extent. They respected her, admired her religious practices which were on par with their own, but found it hard to rise above their own pettiness.

Ambabai kept her home spotlessly clean—washing the frontyard with cowdung water, adorning it with rangoli, watering the tulsi plant every day, performing her elaborate puja, disinfecting the firewood stove. She was a devout woman. Ambabai's benefactor Chikurao Nadiger was a Brahmin and a strict vegetarian. She did not want to hurt his sentiments, and had hence given up cooking and eating non-vegetarian food.

Once it so happened that, clad in her traditional nine-yard sari, she was watering her favourite tulsi plant. An old Brahmin priest was heading back home after a puja at the nearby Venkateshwara Temple. He saw Ambabai and asked her for some water. How could she refuse water to an old man? But how could she hide her caste? Toiling over these thoughts, she had said timidly, "You will not drink water from my hands." The old man replied: "One is Brahmin by deed, not by birth. Go get water and some jaggery."

***

Ambabai was adept at taking down notations. She could put down the *swara*s of any composition while listening to it. She did this often for little Gangu, who had difficulty in capturing the nuances of the songs she heard on the gramophone. In fact, when maestros like Ustad Abdul Karim Khan visited her house, she would quickly write down the notations of the *bandish*es they sang, hoping that some day these would be of use to her dear Gangu.

The story of Ambabai, her mother, grandmother and her daughter contains the stories of hundreds of other women who were remarkably talented but marginalized by history.

Speaking of Gauhar Jan, musicologist Prof. D.P. Mukherjee wrote in an essay for the journal *Sangeet Natak*: "There have been many excellent *khayal* singers among women after Gauhar Jan, but I would feign call[ing] them masters. They are exceedingly competent, but always below the standard that Gauhar Jan occasionally set in *khayal*." In his AIR talk on 7 December 1952, broadcast from Lucknow, he spoke about Gauhar Jan:

> It is a pity that today's world does not know what a great *khayal* singer was lost in the voluptuous folds of *thumri*. Pt. Bhatkhande told me that she was the greatest woman-singer of his time. He must be correct. If you ask me now, I would only place Kesarbai by the side of Gauhar Jan. Kesarbai is the queen of Indian music, as Faiyaz Khan was the king.

In an article on the maverick genius Ustad Vilayat Khan, "The Orthodox Revolutionary", Deepak Raja writes how the great ustad considered Zohrabai Agrewali as a benchmark:

> An important part of Vilayat Khan's vocalized idiom comes from his photographic memory. His study of the *thumri* tradition relied largely on his memory of early twentieth-century gramophone recordings. In October 1991, at a concert in Los Angeles, he reproduced an entire *thumri* rendering of Zohrabai Agrewali ("*Paani bhareri*" in raga Ghara) from a 78-rpm disc, accompanying his sitar rendering with his own voice.

Given the kind of situations these women—Shanmughavadivu, Sunderabai, Begum Akhtar, Bangalore Nagarathnamma, Balasaraswati, Ambabai, Zohrabai—were born into, what they managed to achieve was remarkable. While the men born in that period came to occupy the golden pages of history, the women were relegated to an obscure nook, or forgotten. What makes the lives of these women remarkable and poignant is that they walked untrodden paths not to enter the grand pages of history but only to respect their inner callings. In this regard, the American feminist Elaine Showalter, in her essay "The Female Tradition", said, "[A]ny minority group finds its direction of self-expression in relation to a dominant society." This is usually achieved through the processes of imitation, protest and self-discovery. The extraordinary women of our story chose the third mode. History, geography, incident or locale could only have touched their creative schemes tangentially. Patriarchy, class, caste, empire and nation did play a role, but once they donned their creative selves, they lived a liberated and independent existence.

Of Hirabai, Amarendra Dhaneshwar writes in "Remembering Hirabai" in the journal *Sangeet Natak*:

> N. S. Phadke, a popular novelist of the time was a great fan of Hirabai who was sent to China as a member of the cultural delegation by Jawaharlal Nehru, the first prime minister of India. Phadke wrote in his ornate prose that he loved Hirabai's music so much that he wanted to breathe his last listening to her Bhairavi. "I want to sweeten my last conscious moments listening to her *Jamuna ke teer*."

Hirabai lived at a time when most women musicians came from the class of professional singers belonging to the lower strata of a hierarchical society. Even though they were unmatched in artistry, they could not wipe out the marks of social stigma. In the royal courts, these women—who were as competent as the celebrated ustads—were expected to stand up and sing before the kings. It was only Hirabai's single act of defiance that stopped this custom. In the court of the Nizam of Hyderabad, when she was compelled to stand and perform, she not only refused to sing but also returned the honorarium offered to her.

Ambabai's life, too, is a story of stoic dignity. She was wedded to a Brahmin, but refused to take his name and use it to elevate her social status. Her life also coincides with the tussle that was taking place between modernists or reformers, and traditionalists. New elements were emerging on the national canvas. On the one hand there were the progressives—the Brahmo Samaj, for instance—who took up the cause of the marginalized woman. On the other hand were conservatives who tried hard to preserve a status quo. Both these failed to make a dent in the lives of people like Ambabai. Neither did the reformers come to rescue Ambabai, nor could the traditionalists worsen things for her, for people like Ambabai were neither "modern" as the conservatives understood it, nor were they "traditional" in the parlance of the moderns. Ambabai was a representative of forces that were far too complex and diverse to be understood within such straight-jacketed notions. Women like her tackled history in their own ways, in the process of living out their everyday struggles. She was a pioneer. What she achieved through her daughter Gangubai was to put an end to history's bigoted chapters.

* * *

Ambabai began to look high and low for a guru for her daughter. With the help of her dear friend and mentor Dattopant Desai, they found a teacher in Ganeshpet, Hubli—Hulugooru Krishnamacharya. Dattopant Desai, who could play the dilruba, was a great lover of music. Though he had not undergone any formal training in music, he was an avid listener and had a fair degree of scholarship in music as well. Many musicians came to him for help. Gangubai used to recall how in the large courtyard of Dattopant's house, there used to be a huge coal stove with a big copper pot of milk on slow boil. There would be an endless stream of visitors and musicians flowing into his house, and they could generously help themselves to this milk flavoured with saffron.

He was also a great friend of Sawai Gandharva. As per Dattopant's advice Ambabai decided that Gangubai would seek training from Hulugooru Krishnamacharya. With this find, Ambabai moved out of their Dharwad home and came to live in Hubli. Krishnamacharya took classes in a hall near Ganeshpet. He was a good teacher and taught Gangubai several *bandish*es. She was intelligent and quick to grasp. "When it came to *taal* I was very weak. For several months my mother accompanied me to the class. She would sit behind me playing the tanpura. As she played the tanpura, she gently played the beat on my back, hoping that at least this way I would get a grasp of the rhythm." She learnt her lessons well, but lagged behind in her sense of the *taal*.

Almost after a year, Ambabai went to listen to Gangu and realized that her daughter was still faltering and fumbling with the *taal*. "Gangu is still weak in her rhythm. Maybe you should concentrate on that," Ambabai told Krishnamacharya. Enraged by her comments, he immediately said: "If you pay the fees for an entire year, I will continue to teach, or else look for someone else." This was a big blow! "We had no money on us, where would we get Rs 120 from? It was a very huge sum," Gangubai recalled. There weren't too many music circles and *sabha*s in those days. Both Ambabai and she would get invitations to sing at marriages, pujas, and all kinds of auspicious occasions. But they weren't paid much. However, they considered anything welcome since the going was tough.

There were a few patrons like Nathuram Gokhale, Desai and others who came to their house. If Ambabai sang for them, she got Rs 15. With the money she earned, they barely managed household expenses. Paying Rs 120 for a year was unthinkable. She could have asked her benefactor Chikurao Nadiger, but Ambabai never sought any help.

"My mother had a gold bangle. The only option she had was to sell it. At no cost did she want to stop my music lessons. She sold it and received Rs 100 for it. We were still short of Rs 20—how would we make the rest?" They invited the guru home for lunch and gave him Rs 100 in a plate with coconut, betel leaves and areca nut.

He counted the money and realized it was short of Rs 20. He pushed back the plate and hollered: "Give me Rs 120 or stop coming for lessons!" Ambabai begged him to accept what they had managed to put together: "I will not die without paying your fee gurugale … *oppikollree*, please agree …"

"My guru's ego had been wounded, and had made him heartless at that moment. The episode left a very deep impact on my mind. Whenever I think of that episode, it disturbs me … My mother literally went down on her knees … Exasperated by all this and the difficulty of our lives, I went to a priest who lived behind our house. He was good at astrology and predicted that I would be famous, make money and see better days. Well, things have worked out the way he'd anticipated," Gangubai averred.

She came into her own despite all the bitterness she had experienced in her childhood. In Ganeshpet, the neighbours would interrupt her practice by banging tin containers on the doors. In a manner befitting her nature, she never retaliated. She would steel herself and continue to sing irrespective of the din.

One is reminded of what the great danseuse Balasaraswati would say of Veena Dhanammal, who also came from a family of professional musicians and dancers. When Dhanammal played the veena, everything had to be stopped. There had to be silence. "In the kitchen, even the seasoning wouldn't be prepared because the popping of the mustard seed would disturb grandmother. The washing of clothes—by beating them against stone—had to be halted. We would cease walking around. The people on the street would also become quiet, without any of us having to ask for their cooperation. Vendors would be stopped at the end of the street and told that amma was playing the veena and that they should return later." Gangubai was incapable of such an authoritative nature. She just bore all her difficulties without a whimper and soldiered on.

In an early autobiography of Gangubai, *Nanna Badukina Haadu*, narrated by the Kannada writer N.K. Kulkarni, she says: "My life has many such bitter incidents, but I don't think I should speak about them and make this reading experience unpleasant for you. Anyway, the same people who treated me badly and threw me out of their houses came back to me with respect later in my life. They invited me to lunch, dinner … and showered praises on me. How strange this world is!"

* * *

Lessons with Hulugooru Krishnamacharya could not go on for very long. Gangubai had learnt about thirty to forty *bandish*es from him and Ambabai began to feel that her daughter needed a more proficient teacher. The search started all over again. Ambabai confided in Dattopant: she wanted Gangu to learn from a good guru. The person Dattopant immediately thought of was his friend, the torchbearer of Kirana *gharana,* Sawai Gandharva.

Karim's reham, Gandharva's grace

The unparalleled maestro of Kirana *gharana,* Sawai Gandharva's name was Ramachandra Kundagolkar. He later acquired the title Sawai Gandharva ("Sawai" translates as "one and a quarter" in Marathi), which came to be his name for the rest of his life. He was the prized disciple of Ustad Abdul Karim Khan, the founder of Kirana *gharana*, and extended his teacher's style by bringing his own elements into it with his innovative genius.

Ramachandra's father was an accountant at the Wade (the house of the richest landholder in the village) in Kundagol taluk, a quiet, sleepy taluk, twenty kilometres from Hubli. Agriculture was the chief profession of the people there, who grew mainly chillies and areca. Ganesh Samshi, Ramachandra's father, worked at the Wade of Ranganagowda Nadiger, one of the biggest landlords of Kundagol in those times. The little one often tagged along with his father on his way to the Wade and played around, but through all his activities he would hum constantly, all day long. Ganesh Samshi put his son in school and nurtured dreams of his son becoming a big officer. Ramachandra went to school, of course, but would unfailingly stop at every temple on the way, and would never tire of listening to bhajans and *kirtan*s sung there. He would amble to school slowly, singing what he had heard.

His teachers were also so fond of his sweet, fluid voice that they never punished the musically preoccupied Ramachandra. In fact, they often asked him to sings songs and recite poems. Each time there was an inspection at the school, he would easily impress the inspectors with his music. With his heart firmly set on music, he hardly had a clue about his lessons. If at all he got promoted to the next class, it was due to his music.

Things got more interesting for Ramachandra when he had to go to the Lamington High School in Hubli. He had a great time watching all the plays that visited Hubli and always dreamt of seeing himself on stage, singing the wonderful *natyasangeet.* On one such occasion, he was fortunate to hear Abdul Karim Khan saab's concert in Hubli, and was charmed by his serene music. After that, there was only one burning desire in Ramachandra's heart: to become a pupil of the maestro.

It became increasingly difficult for Ganesh Samshi to send his son to school. He could not afford it. Sending him to Hubli would be too heavy on his pocket. Ramachandra's schooling was abruptly interrupted, and the boy went back to accompanying his father to the Wade. The Nadiger noticed how Samshi's son could think of nothing beyond music, and strongly felt that the boy's innate talent must not be allowed to wither away. He advised Samshi to get his son musically trained. As luck would have it, Balvantrao Kolhatkar had come to live in Kundagol. He became Ramachandra's teacher. The Nadigers, who were great lovers of music, were an extremely generous and charitable family: they indulged Ramachandra's musical talent.

Ramachandra's music lessons continued uninterruptedly till his teacher's sudden death in 1898. The young boy was bereft, and missed his teacher sorely. Just a few months later, Abdul Karim Khan saab came to stay at the Wade en route from Mysore to Miraj. The ustad had developed a fondness for the Nadiger family, and often stopped by to enjoy several weeks of hospitality at the Wade. Ramachandra was on tenterhooks each time Khan saab made a stopover. Thinking of the ustad's concert he had heard in Hubli left him with goosebumps. He restlessly hovered around the ustad and desperately tried to hold on to every little inadvertent note that escaped Khan saab's mouth. One day, as he sat in one of the corners of the huge, sprawling Wade, trying to recapture the brilliance of Khan saab's remarkable rendition of the Bhairavi *bandish Jamuna ke Teer*, Khan saab's attention fell on the young lad. Impressed by the young boy's talent, he made him sing. Not only did he recognize Ramachandra's enormous potential to be a competent musician, he also sensed his deep passion for music. Khan saab offered to take him as his disciple. In 1901, Ramachandra became the disciple of Karim Khan saab, but not before Khan saab took an undertaking from the family that the boy would spend a minimum of eight years with him, undisturbed.

Ramachandra's life took a dramatic turn at this point, and what happened eventually occupies history's most celebrated pages. Like any other gurukul, life at Khan saab's house came with its set of duties. Apart from rigorous music lessons, he had to put in his share of household chores.

Abdul Karim Khan was an innovator with a highly original mind. His music, characterized by sweetness, was completely stripped of jerky movements and conflicts. Since it had its roots in the sarangi and veena played by his forefathers, Khan saab's vocalism paid great attention to the refinement of *swara* and *shruti.* There are enchanting stories of how the resonance of the tanpuras tuned by him was such that one could just listen to it for hours on end. There is yet another story of Khan saab at a concert accompanied by four tanpuras: when the *madhyam* of one of the tanpuras sank, he, without batting an eyelid, turned around and put his finger on the exact tanpura.

Khan saab was deeply influenced by the Carnatic style of singing. His musical beliefs were so egalitarian that he never hesitated to borrow from other styles of music to enrich his own. He recast the borrowed elements to suit the Kirana style. In one of his earliest rpm recordings, where he renders Carnatic ragas, he even sings *kalpanaswara*s, something he was completely opposed to. Referring to the *swara prasthaara*, he would say, "Carnatic musicians play harmonium with their mouth!" But if he did change his opinion about this aspect of Carnatic music, it was due to Veena Dhanammal. Khan saab, who would camp at her house during his visits to Madras, had great regard for her artistry. Contemporary musicologists, such as Tirukkadikkaval Krishna

Iyer, are supposed to have said: "For Dhanammal's music one can forsake all the fourteen worlds!" In a later recording, Khan saab sang "*Rama Nee Samanamevaru*" in Kharaharapriya and "*Entha Nerchina*" in Saveri. It was a great tribute to the consummate artistry of Veena Dhanammal. It was also a salute to the path she chose in order to rise above her social circumstances. Khan saab's tribute was, in a way, to all the remarkable women of those times.

Under the tutelage of Ustad Abdul Karim Khan, Ramachandra studied music all day—morning, afternoon and evening. Khan saab, who was not an advocate of a vast repertoire, believed in pristine perfection. For an entire year, Ramachandra practised only raga Pooriya. This disciple, who was ready for any amount of hard work, would ungrudgingly do everything that his teacher asked him to do. Khan saab did not believe in keeping a book and taking down notes or notations. He believed music had to be etched in the minds and so his theory lessons were never separate from the vocal lessons.

When Ramachandra turned sixteen, a great calamity befell him. Common to boys of that age, his voice cracked and with it everything altered, especially the range and fluidity of his voice. His voice turned hoarse, nearly shattering all his dreams. However, the ustad who had made pioneering efforts in voice culture stood firm. He took Ramachandra through a long journey of *sur sadhana.* As was his nature, Ramachandra put in all his might. It was difficult, there were many trying moments, but Khan saab wasn't the kind to give up. Such love towards a student is rare. Apparently, it took Khan saab a good seven years to bring the voice back to shape. During this period, neither the ustad nor the disciple lost faith or determination.

Despite his lifelong dedication to music, his voice was never compliant. Sawai Gandharva would begin practising four to five hours ahead of his performance so that it would reach an appropriate form by the time of the performance. His voice was unpredictable and often gave him apprehensions, but once it came into form, there was no looking back.

His student Firoze Dastur would often narrate a charming episode about the whimsical nature of his Guruji's voice to the musicologist Kumar Prasad Mukherji.

> Suppose there was Guruji's concert at Laxmibai Hall, we friends would settle down with cups of tea and chat at the Chowpatty beach. Our man would be posted at the hall. At around seven, a good hour after the concert had started, he would come speeding on the bicycle, furiously ringing the bell and shouting, *'Lag gaya, sur lag gaya.'* We would then rush to the hall and find people pouring in, and in no time it would be brimming over with a crowd. Once Rambhauji started singing, there was no stopping him. He could sing for five hours at a stretch.

Ramachandra, hungry to expand his knowledge, sought training under Bhaskarbua Bakhle, Nisar Hussain Khan, Rahim Bux and other senior artistes of the time. This he did much to the chagrin of Khan saab. In eight years, Khan saab taught him only three ragas—*Todi*, *Multani* and *Pooriya.* But he learnt other ragas from various gurus. Ramachandra was a man of remarkable commitment: Khan saab would be annoyed when Ramachandra paid due credit to his other teachers, but that did not stop him from doing so. His relationship with Khan saab was one of unswerving devotion, and Khan saab was aware of it: it remained unchanged till the guru's death in 1937.

Ramachandra was his most cherished disciple. He managed to blend the styles of other *gharana*s without moving away from the Kirana *gharana* tradition. Hence, the style shaped by Ramachandra had *boltaan*, *murki*s, *badhat* and the gushing *taan*s. Ramachandra's voice did not have the spontaneity and mobility of Khan saab, but it had his unmistakable signature. Dedication towards one's disciples was part of the legacy handed down by Khan saab to Ramachandra.

Ramachandra could not contain his temptation for theatre: Marathi theatre was at its peak at that time. The family eagerly hoped that Ramachandra would now support them and bail them out of their difficulties. In 1907, he joined Marathi theatre for a salary of Rs 100. Even this was not something Khan saab appreciated. He did not relish the fact that a competent musician of the *gharana* was donning female roles and singing *natyasangeet.* It was Ramachandra's longstanding dream, however, and his sound classical training obviously made his *natyasangeet* renditions remarkable. His singing was imbued with a feminine charm, which not only made his renditions extremely pleasing but also worked to his advantage in the female roles he played. Ramachandra had precise timing, with which he brilliantly interspersed melody and rhythm. He became a phenomenal success.

Having heard about the immense popularity of his disciple, Karim Khan saab turned up at one of his performances. It was the play *Saubhadra*. Ramachandra in his sari walked on to the stage with the swing and grace of a woman, and was horror-struck to see Karim Khan saab in the very first row itself! His throat went dry, and his mind blank. But with a packed hall, he could not even take his time to recover. At the end of the play, Ramachandra had changed his guru's perceptions. His renditions were so inspiring that even Abdul Karim Khan saab felt compelled to learn *natyasangeet.* In the years to follow, he sang a couple of stage songs like "*Prema Seva Sharan*" and "*Nach Sundari Karu Kopa*".

Alongside his theatre expeditions, Ramachandra continued to give classical music concerts. He did *riyaz* regularly and sang for small *baithak*s. That's probably why, even after he gave up theatre, he could go back to singing Hindustani classical full-time. People had not forgotten him as a serious practitioner of *khayal.* It is to his credit that he managed to excel during the time of the legendary Bal Gandharva, who had been the undisputed king of Marathi theatre for nearly five decades. Ramachandra not only measured up to this iconic figure, but was on par with him. In fact, it is said that aficionados bought tickets to both their play performances, and would watch the first half of Bal Gandharva's play and rush to catch the second half of Sawai Gandharva's.

In 1919, the two great musicians came to camp together at Amaravathi. And as chance would have it, both their plays were based on Draupadi's *vastrapaharana,* her disrobing by the Kaurava camp. Ramachandra played Atmateja, Bal Gandharva played Draupadi. The audience feasted on the songs and at the end of the two performances, Dadasaheb Kharpade, a wealthy patron, conferred the title Sawai Gandharva on Ramachandra, which came to stay as his name, in the latter half of his musical career.

After 1931, Sawai Gandharva stopped singing for Marathi theatre. He got back to full-fledged concert singing and came to be in great demand. He was giving concerts all over Maharashtra, was recording for All India Radio, and, come Ganesh Puja, he would have concerts every single day of the week in Bombay. He was among the few gifted artistes who could sing a raga for more than two hours. In the true Kirana style, he emphasized every single note and meditated on it, revealing its many contours. Even after listening to his music for hours, people would still be willing to listen to more.

At the peak of his career, on one of his visits to Kundagol, the meticulous Dattopant Desai took Gangubai to meet him. He listened to the young girl's music, and was impressed, but expressed his inability to teach her since he was constantly in and out of Kundagol on concert tours. "That's perfectly alright. Teach her whenever you are here," Dattopant urged. That came to be the arrangement for the next few years: She took lessons when he had no concert at hand.

By 1936, Sawai Gandharva put a check on his concerts, and came to spend longer periods at Kundagol. This not only heralded a new chapter for Gangubai, but also for Sawai Gandharva. His role as a teacher par excellence began at this point. He offered to the country the century's two outstanding musicians: Bhimsen Joshi and Gangubai Hangal. Kundagol became a prominent place on the cultural map of the country. Bhimsen Joshi and Gangubai gave it salience strictly within the Kirana framework.

Vamanrao Deshpande, in his book *Between Two Tanpuras,* observes that, in the Kirana *gharana*, each generation imported new ideas and yet the basic characteristics of the *gharana* remained inviolable. Abdul Karim Khan concentrated on *sur,* while Sawai Gandharva's presentation was more organized and rhythm-based, and Bhimsen Joshi brought rhythm even into the *vilambit* portion. Gangubai's music lacked the feminine grace and lyricism of its founder, but she infused it with a rugged power and an unusual devotion that was true of her guru's music as well.

* * *

During 1930-31, thanks to Dattopant Desai's persuasive powers, the constantly travelling Sawai Gandharva relented to teach Gangubai, even if intermittently. A *Ganda Bandhan* ceremony was organized at their Hubli house, a *gurudakshina* was offered and Gangubai finally became the student of Sawai Gandharva formally. What went on to become a great relationship of commitment, started with a composition in raga *Yaman*—"*Guru Bin Kaise Gun Gave*"—which also became the refrain of Gangubai's life.

Sawai Gandharva was very sensitive to the requirements of every individual voice. Having undergone years of trauma himself, he asked Gangubai to do intense *kharaj sadhana. Kharaj*, the notes of the lower octave, would strengthen her base voice. Sawai Gandharva had such a clear picture of what he was doing that nothing could alter his plans. There were times when he taught just two notes and they had to be repeated several times a day. He would not teach anything else for the next couple of weeks, sometimes he would stretch it to months.

"I would get bored. I often grumbled, sulked and complained to my mother," Gangubai told me. Ambabai coaxed her daughter to be patient, for that was the only way notes could be mastered.

When Sawai Gandharva embarked on his concert tours, Gangu's lessons were put on hold. Sometimes his theatre company (by this time he had set up his own company) camped for several days in Hubli. Then, Ambabai would ask Dattopant to request Guruji to have his music rehearsals in their house itself. The lady was so committed to the future of her daughter that she carefully listened to Guruji's singing during the rehearsals. Gangu, of course, fixed herself before him, rapt and completely absorbed. Ambabai, with pen and paper in hand, would busily take down notations, follow his raga treatment and the way he dealt with rhythm—she sopped up every single detail. Dattopant was always there with her. Once Sawai Gandharva left for his theatrical expeditions Gangu's practice was monitored by Dattopant and Ambabai. "No, no, that is not the way Guruji held that note", "Oh Gangu, you have to refine that phrase, your *madhyam* is not matching up"—in this manner Dattopant and Ambabai would monitor her with great care. Ramanna, Ambabai's brother and Gangu's maternal uncle, was well-versed with the tabla. He used to accompany her in her practice.

By the time Gangubai came to her fourth standard, she realized that her heart was not in her studies. She was deeply into music and could think of nothing else but that. She was very quick with languages and knew Kannada and Marathi extremely well. Even though she loved books and read voraciously, school was not something that interested her. Ambabai didn't push her daughter either, instead she allowed her to live in her world of music. Working hard to support her school and music, and to keep their life going, was not easy on Ambabai. Hence, when her daughter expressed her desire to leave school, she relented.

* * *

Years passed, and Gururaj Kaulgi came along. He was a great admirer of music who often came by to listen to the music of Ambabai and Gangubai. This Brahmin widower was a law graduate from the University of Bombay. After a couple of visits, he expressed his desire to marry Gangubai. "I was a little over fifteen then. My mother fixed the marriage. But when I got a chance to speak to him, he told me that his parents wanted him to remarry in his own caste. I thought it was only fair that they felt that way. I told him to marry the girl of his parents' choice, and if there was still space for me, I told him I could come in after that," she had said in a matter-of-fact manner.

Gangubai was a woman of no confusion: she knew her social standing and did not seek to violently change it. All her dilemmas were mostly artistic. With the help of a strong backing from her mother, she silently but steadily steered her life away from traditional *devadasi* practices. She was fully aware that there were some things that couldn't be changed or overlooked in her lifetime—for instance, her caste. She had, however, become a stepping stone to transformation for the coming generation.

So, Kaulgi got married to his sister's daughter, as per his parents' wish. His heart beat for Gangubai, and he couldn't think of being separated from her. He married her as well. Gangubai married Kaulgi as per the tradition of her caste—with the tanpura beside her. Marriage, of course, didn't mean moving to her husband's home—there was no societal consent for this. She continued to stay with her mother and carried on with her music lessons. Her father Chikurao Nadiger didn't seem to play a major role in their lives. He visited them often, took stock of their lives, and returned to his Ranebennur home. As far as responsibility was concerned, he never took any. Gangubai never complained about it and neither did her mother. But the good-natured man that Nadiger was, he did express happiness over his daughter's marriage. "Whenever my father came to our house from Ranebennur, I would invariably be sitting with the tanpura. 'What is this, Gangu, you are forever singing. Wont you take a break and talk to me?' he would chide me affectionately. He was a soft-spoken, loving person …"

Within a year of Gangubai's marriage to Kaulgi, a daughter was born to her—Krishna. The young girl of sixteen now had a baby to take care of. She used to put Krishna in a cloth cradle and hang it from the ceiling. She would rock the cradle with one hand, hold the tanpura with the other, and practise her music. Those were the days when Mallikarjun Mansur was back to singing at the theatre company. After his rehearsals, he would invariably stop over at Gangubai's house. He would hold Krishna, cuddle and pamper her, and play with her. He never left without singing to her. "You go," he would tell Gangubai, "I will play with Kitti." And while Gangubai went about finishing her chores, Mansur would rock baby Krishna in the cloth cradle, he would curl up and sleep right under it. For the rest of his life, Mansur had a soft corner for Krishna. When Mansur was on his deathbed, Gangubai went to see him at the hospital. He was very ill and could barely respond. Bending over him, she whispered into his ears: *Mallanna, Mallanna ... naanu bandidini Mallanna ... kannu bittu nodu Mallanna* ... she urged him to open his eyes and see her. Mallanna slowly moved his eyelids and, with great difficulty, managed to part his lips. All that he could say was *ta* ... *ta* ... she was his fond *tangi* (sister).

In 1932, Gangubai was carrying her second child. In the same year Ambabai also fell seriously ill. She was diagnosed with stomach ulcers and had to undergo surgery. However, the doctors told her that it was not an emergency, and she could wait for six months before undergoing the surgery. Ambabai wouldn't listen. She had her own plans. "After six months? It will not be possible. That's the time Gangu will have her baby, and I have to be at her service. Else, who will nurse the mother and the baby?" She was worried also that it might disrupt Gangubai's music lessons that were just about moving towards stability. Ambabai underwent the surgery almost immediately, but unfortunately there was a rupture in the stitches made, which led to excessive bleeding—Ambabai didn't survive. Gangubai was shattered. "Imagine my life without my mother … she was the breath of my life … I stopped singing."

Chikurao Nadiger came rushing from Ranebennur for the last rites. He was heartbroken. Overcome by the grief of Ambabai's death, the man lost interest in everything. He did not live for long after that, and was gone in a year. Without much emphasis on meaning or intent, Gangubai had narrated the following episode: "A few months ahead of my mother's death, an astrologer had come to our doorstep. He predicted that my father would lose his wife. On hearing this, my mother was grief-stricken. She worried endlessly about how my father would manage with his wife gone. She often expressed her anxiety to me. But it was my mother who died."

Just before Ambabai's death, HMV had come to the south, exploring voices that could be recorded. They had asked Gangubai to sing for them and had even fixed a future date. Ambabai's death had, however, left her in no state of mind to render even a single note. She flatly refused and asked for her contract to be cancelled. Dattopant and Ramanna stood by her like solid pillars. They gently coaxed her to sing, and kept consoling her. In fact, every morning Dattopant would arrive at their house. The first thing he would do was to tune the tanpura, and then would keep strumming it. He hoped that the resonating drone of the tanpura would fill both house and heart, and Gangu would get back to her music. It was not easy. This went on for months, and Dattopant did not give up. Ramanna, too, had to join Dattopant. As he ran his fingers on the tanpura, Ramanna would keep the rhythm. Before Dattopant's silent persistence, Gangu's obduracy seemed frail. "I eventually realized that music was the only way to keep my mother in my thoughts constantly. She always dreamt of making me a great musician. And Dattopant was always around to share her dream. I gave up mourning, picked up my tanpura and started practising."

Life had to go on. There were practical, everyday questions that had to be addressed. What would help put food on their plates if she stopped singing? She was a school dropout, and music was her only route to survival. There were occasional requests for her to sing at small gatherings, family functions or festivals. There used to be a Saturday *baithak* at their home as long as Ambabai lived. There was a regular, small audience for the *baithak.* Even during the period of Gangubai's mourning, they came, sat for a while, and left some money for her. In her later years, she would recall all these gestures with immense gratitude. As soon as she realized that she had to resume singing, she shouldered the Saturday *baithak*s. With the little money she earned, the family pulled along with great difficulty.

"During the first death anniversary, family members are supposed to give away a sari to a *sumangali* (a lady whose husband is alive). My mother's death anniversary approached, and my condition was appalling. I had no money, not even a few rupees to buy an ordinary sari. Dattopant knew. He did not even ask. On that day, he placed a sari in my hands. I was so moved by this gesture, I could not stop crying. His affection was so selfless. You think I would have been all this without the unconditional love I received from people like Dattopant? He was always there for me ..." Gangubai would say, sobbing uncontrollably.

It was time for her to go to Bombay for her recording with HMV. "My mother had so many dreams for this day. It was my very first recording and she was not a part of it." She left for Bombay with Dattopant and Ramanna. She had no money to buy herself a new sari. She gave her everyday saris an extra-good wash, pressed them under a pillow and took them along. On their way they stopped at Pune, and paid a brief visit to her guru, Sawai Gandharva. Gangubai presented before him all the eleven songs that she was to sing at the recording. Sawai Gandharva listened carefully, and gave them the necessary polish.

Both in Pune and Bombay, people made rude remarks about her clothes. Gangubai had no illusions about her looks or clothes. With music being the mission of her life, she was in no position to take these comments seriously. She wasn't even the kind who would return those taunts. "I would just laugh and keep quiet."

Gangubai enjoyed her Bombay trip thoroughly. Along with other artistes from various parts of the country, she was stationed at a hotel in Girgaon. Each of them had to present a set of eleven songs, and it had to be an eclectic selection. Gangubai presented her compositions. There were pieces in ragas *Natakuranji* and *Madhyamavati*, taught to her by her mother, alongwith Marathi *natyasangeet*, also composed by her mother. She sang *Miyan ki Malhar* along with the other pieces. "We were not paid for this. However, they took care of our travel, accommodation and food, and even took us around Bombay. It was the beginning of many things for me."

On this very first trip Gangubai gained the confidence of the recording company. G.N. Joshi, who was a visionary in the recording industry in India, was the manager of HMV. He was a singer as well. In fact, around the time that Gangubai was there for her recording, his recording was also scheduled. The female singer who was supposed to record a Marathi duet with him failed to grasp the tune despite repeated attempts. Gangubai, who entered the studio at that very moment, was asked to give it a go. Her principles did not allow her to agree, and she knew that the other artiste would feel hurt. But the lady readily gave her consent. Gangubai tried, and the very first take was accepted. Everyone in the studio was elated.

The first trip was followed by a second one in no time. But no trip to Bombay could be undertaken without paying a visit to her guru in Pune. She had to record classical this time, and therefore planned a longer stay in Pune with long and rigorous practice sessions. Gangubai was paid for this recording. "Do you know how D.V. Paluskar referred to the fee? He called it *sakshatkar* (realization). 'The concert was fine, but the *sakshatkar* was not so fine,' he would say," Gangubai would laugh recalling this, showing off the only two teeth left in her mouth.

Gangubai recorded her first set with HMV under the name Gangubai Hublikar. The logic was simple: she came from Hubli and hence her second name was Hublikar. But her older maternal uncle Krishnappa took serious objection to this. "Why Hubli? Isn't Hangal our ancestral place? Do you feel ashamed because it's a village? Are you so big a star that you no longer want to belong to a village but to a town?" During the second round of recordings, she told the recording company to change her second name to Hangal. Well, they did, but with that they changed her first name as well. This time they called her Gandhari Hangal! "I've no clue why they changed my name! Maybe they thought my name was too old-fashioned. Hee … hee …" she grinned.

After this recording, there was a music festival in Bombay. Many leading artistes of the country, Ustad Vilayat Hussain Khan, Manji Khan and others, had been invited to sing at the programme. By the time the last artiste's performance was over it was well past 2 a.m. The artiste's as well as the audience had no choice but to stay on till the local trains resumed in the morning. Seeing Gangubai in the audience, the organizers, who knew her, forced her to sing. "I am a newcomer and cannot sing before these ustads," she pleaded. But eventually she had to sing. The *Miyan ki Malhar* she sang that day left an indelible mark on everyone's memory, so much so that it changed the course of her musical career for good.

All India Radio had just then been set up in 1936. During one of Gangubai's visits to Bombay, Hirabai Badodekar had a recording at AIR. But at the time of recording, Hirabai took ill suddenly and the authorities panicked. Hirabai asked Gangubai to sing in her place. At this concert, All India Radio announced her name as Gangubai Hangal, and that came to stay. All confusion regarding her name was put to rest permanently.

Echoes of the invisible world

"Music has only history, and no geography," Gangubai often said. She had mentioned this in a different context, but this is precisely how All India Radio brought together the culture and heritage of the country. It unified the people of the country in a way no other medium could. While it safeguarded the rich cultural heritage of the country not overlooking its diversity, it transmitted important voices from one corner of the country to another.

Former director general of All India Radio, U.L. Baruah, in his 1983 book *This Is All India Radio*, quotes an earlier director general J.C. Mathur: "When radio came on the Indian scene in the thirties, music was already on the lookout for new patronage." Mathur continues this thought in *Aspects of Indian Music*, where he places the rising popularity of radio in context:

> As a result of the new economic impact, the princes and landlords gradually ceased to be patrons of music. Theatre had been unceremoniously jettisoned by cinema. Though the early films made use of classical melodies, it was very clear from the very beginning that this new form of entertainment would not have much use for traditional and classical music, and would depend on other devices for enlivening its presentation.

However, the gramophone continued. Although the long-playing record was still far off, old masters continued to derive some income, but less satisfaction from the brief recordings they were able to give. In such a situation, it was doubtful whether high-brow Indian music could survive as a form of art and entertainment. It was then that the radio came to the scene with its offer of opportunities to both the old masters and promising young artistes. Musicians could now give freer play to their art and reach the homes of the people in their hours of leisure.

In his history of the radio, Baruah notes that broadcasting in many countries in the world had begun in the early 1920s itself. In India, however, this institution developed only in the latter half of the 1920s, and, this too, due to the efforts of amateur enterprises. "Organized broadcasting," he says, "began when the first station of Indian Broadcasting Company was inaugurated at [sic] Bombay by the British viceroy of India, Lord Irwin, on 23 July 1927. Five weeks later, on 26 August 1927, the Calcutta station was inaugurated by the governor of Bengal."

In September 1935, broadcasting began in the princely state of Mysore with the name "Akashavani". Dr M.V. Gopalaswamy, a professor of psychology at the University of Mysore, started this enterprise from his home. When the Mysore state realized the nature of its reach, it took over the enterprise six years later, in 1941.

Meanwhile, radio stations came into existence in other parts of the country. On 1 January 1936, the Delhi station was also launched. It was due to the insistence of the controller Lionel Fielden that the name All India Radio came to stay. In his autobiography, *The Natural Bent*, Fielden records the travails of the early years of broadcasting. He delineates the purpose of All India Radio in broad and clear terms. Along with the name "All India Radio", Gopalaswamy's "Akashavani" also came to stay.

No sooner did AIR come into existence, than it launched a survey which would help charter a course and envision what the audiences required. A survey done in 1936 found that Indian classical music evoked a response of 30 per cent. But in 1938, when All India Radio, Madras, came into existence, the response for Indian classical music was 60 per cent. So a large chunk of All India Radio's programmes was music. Even as the trend waned steadily in the later years, for the longest time All India Radio as an institution did believe that its motto was "service" and "preservation". To this day, AIR boasts of the richest music archives. It was mandatory for every station to develop its own distinct personality in accordance with the cultural traditions of the region. At the same time, it also gave the regional artistes a national presence and identity.

It was properly coincidental that the beginning of Gangubai's career as a classical musician and the early years of broadcasting happened together in India. It was in the early 1930s that she started making trips to Bombay for HMV recordings. At that point, All India Radio was young and enthusiastic. Gangubai was invited to sing at its various stations. When she had more time to focus on classical music, she gave up singing *natyasangeet*, *thumri*, *ghazal*, *bhavageethe* and devotional music.

It was around the same time that Sawai Gandharva also returned to settle down in Kundagol, this time to don the role of a full-time guru. By 1931, Sawai Gandharva, after having suffered huge financial losses with his theatre company, decided to wind it up. He bid a final goodbye to theatre. By 1936-37, he managed to operate from Kundagol despite being busy with numerous concerts.

This was a hectic period in Gangubai's personal life as well. All her three children were born by then. She had started making frequent trips to Bombay, even as her lessons at Kundagol continued in full swing. Ramanna's family had also expanded and Gangubai's responsibilities had spiralled. She had many mouths to feed. "I was paid Rs 50 then. For Ramanna and me, the to and fro train ticket to Bombay would cost Rs 9. We would spend three to four rupees on food and other things. I would be left with Rs 37. Tell me, how does one manage with such a paltry income, and with so many people at home? Sometimes hungry, sometimes half-hungry, sometimes just a loaf of bread for all of us—each day came with a new challenge," she recalled.

The year 1936 was significant for Gangubai as an artiste. Her first full-fledged AIR programme was broadcast live from the Bombay station. AIR was flooded with letters, everyone wanting to know more about this singer. Each letter that flowed in from various parts of the state had extolled her virtuous *Miyan ki Malhar,* which had an unmistakable stamp of the Kirana *gharana.* With this overwhelming response, AIR accorded prestige to Gangubai's singing with them. Hence, performing for All India Radio became a regular feature after this point. Singing for the radio was a matter of great satisfaction: one did not have to pack everything into three minutes—a tough demand that the gramophone made on performers. But this was not easy either. While it gave the musician the freedom and luxury of time, Gangubai realized that she had to step up her *riyaz.* Her lessons had to become more serious and exacting.

All India Radio had a unique policy: every Hindustani musician who came into a particular station for recording had to present three ragas belonging to three different *prahar*s (times of the day). All performing artistes were also required to send a list of twenty-five ragas that they wished to sing in their future recordings. Gangubai recalled that this was very challenging and daunting for a musician, at least for those who were just about finding their feet in the world of music.

"I was extremely nervous. It was a test of my ability. I was already spending ten hours on my *riyaz,* it was difficult for me to increase the number of hours. My lessons had to be more frequent. It was worrying me." Apart from making subtle requests to her guru through Ramanna and Dattopant, she began to scavenge bookshops for a copy of Bhatkhande's book on Hindustani ragas. She managed to procure a copy and plunged into a serious study of it. Astute and hardworking, Gangubai was not the kind to rest her entire faith in music theory. "Even after all my intense study of Bhatkhande, my knowledge was only bookish. A book can only take you some distance. There is no substitute for a guru or *sadhana*," she had said, lying down on her bed and looking far away.

In those early years, she once had to give two performances for AIR at very short notice. She had barely finished one recording, and she got summons for the next. In the throes of panic she chose Bibhas, a morning raga. This raga had not been taught to her but was something that she had learnt on her own. There wasn't a chance she could sing it before her guru, for he was away on a concert tour. Since she couldn't consult him, she also took solace in the fact that he was away and wouldn't listen to her programme when it went on air. And even if he did come back in time for the broadcast, there was no electricity in Kundagol and there was no way he could listen to her rendition of Bibhas.

Gangubai left for Bombay, recorded Bibhas successfully, and took the next train back to Hubli. She had barely stepped into the train, when something happened to her—she became cold and numb. She couldn't move. Ramanna, who stood behind her with all their luggage, waiting to get in, got impatient with her and urged her to move, "*Ey ... mundakka hoga Gangu ...* Come on, move in," but she wouldn't. Ramanna literally pushed her inside and got in. He looked in the direction in which Gangubai's gaze was fixed, and straight across, in the very same compartment sat Guru Sawai Gandharva! She hadn't expected to see him there, and was shocked to find him. Both Ramanna and Gangu were at a total loss for words. After a couple of minutes, gathering herself, she sheepishly walked up to him, touched his feet and turned to go back to her seat. "Gangu," he called, waving her over to his side. Her legs shaking with fear, she sat down beside him. "Where are you coming from, Guruji?" she managed to ask. "I had a concert in Bombay," he replied in a matter-of-fact way. He was looking out of the window as she sat beside him meekly. The train began to move. "So … where are you coming from?" he asked. Gangubai fell silent. Not a word came out, much as she tried. "What was that raga you sang on the radio?" he quietly asked, turning to his dear disciple sitting beside him like a tiny, little sparrow. She had been praying hard so this topic wouldn't come up and lo it had! Sensing his unusually nonchalant tone, Gangu instantly knew something was dramatically wrong.

"Well … it was … it was …"

"It was what?"

"*Bibhas*, Guruji," she managed to say, swallowing lumps that stuck like boulders in her throat.

"You call that *Bibhas*? Which *gharana* sings it that way? In our *gharana* we use the *komal dhaivat* and not *teevra dhaivat* that you employed."

There was silence. "So many mistakes even in your *Megh Malhar*!" She was on the verge of weeping.

"Can't you ask me before going public? People all over the country listen to the radio and they will hold me responsible for all the mistakes you made," he thundered. Gangubai was sad that she had done a bad job, but also wondered what her fellow passengers would think of this huge drama.

"Don't put me through this agony, Gangu!" he hollered yet again. Sawai Gandharva was livid.

There was no conversation for a while, like the calm after a storm. Gangu felt as if someone had stuck her on that seat. She had no courage to go back to her seat next to Ramanna. After a few minutes, he ordered, "Where's your tanpura? Get it." He tuned the tanpura, made himself comfortable and started singing Bibhas. The fellow passengers felt sufficiently amused and entertained with what was unfolding before them. Gangu was embarrassed. But Sawai Gandharva was absolutely serious. He was engrossed in Bibhas and did not register anything else that happened around him. Gradually, Gangubai also joined him. In the next few moments, they were both lost to the world. Ramanna walked up and quietly sat beside them. In a little while, the fellow passengers gave up their amusement. The journey from Bombay to Kundagol had nothing else for Sawai Gandharva and Gangubai but the pursuit of Bibhas. When they disembarked the train to the familiar sounds of the Hubli railway station, Gangubai wondered if it had been a reverie.

This uncompromising pursuit of perfection on the part of Sawai Gandharva led to the making of disciples like Gangubai. His approach was slow, but he believed in excellence. In her later years, Gangubai would always remember this, "He may have taught us very few ragas, but the manner in which he taught us prepared us to handle any raga."

Many years later, when Sawai Gandharva was very ill and stayed with Gangubai, he could not stop himself from teaching her. She would sit down to practise in her room, and with great difficulty the feeble and frail guru would walk to her room and sit down to correct her. Gangubai was always moved to tears whenever she recalled the times she spent with her guru. Sawai Gandharva lived and breathed music, and he passed on the fervour to his students. If all her life she stood solidly like a rock, unswayed by fame or money even in the face of adversity, it was not just her personal belief, but also the schooling of a guru like Sawai Gandharva.

* * *

By the end of 1936, Gangubai's lessons were streamlined. Sawai Gandharva came to stay in Kundagol and she started making everyday trips for her lessons. There were trains leaving Hubli that passed through Kundagol. She took the train along with Dattopant Desai in the initial days, but later it was her maternal uncle Ramanna who became her guardian angel. It took them an hour by train, and from there it was a fairly long walk to Sawai Gandharva's house.

The walk to her guru's house was far more arduous than her musical journey itself. People rushed out of their homes and jeered at her: "Look, look, there goes the *gaanewaali*!" They would hurl objects at her and pass rude, abusive remarks. These were moments of great humiliation for the young Gangubai. In the initial days, she would cringe and stick to Ramanna, and the minute she reached Guruji's house, she would collapse on the stone bench outside and shed silent tears. Ramanna would put a comforting arm around the shoulders of his young niece and both of them would sit there quietly, trying to recover from those horrifying moments. Somehow Guruji always sensed that Gangu had come for her lessons. He would go out himself, hold her hand, and take her in. Many a time he would just stand by the stone bench in silence and wait for Gangu to recover. "Music is your life's mission. It must give you the strength to face everything else," Sawai Gandharva would say, beginning his lessons for the day. Of course, there was no ready prescription for this, she had to brew her own concoction. Gangubai learnt her lessons of loneliness rather early.

As days passed, Gangubai learnt to put her head down, steel herself, turn a deaf ear to all that was being said about her, and take bold steps to Guru Sawai Gandharva's house. Ramanna, who walked by her side, would try to catch his dear Gangu's expression from the corner of his eye. But her gaze was fixed on the ground and her heart on music. He could feel the power of her conviction. The resolve to master music was so sturdy that even the meanest slander couldn't weaken it. Till her very end, Gangubai fortified her music from every force, and guarded the purity of her music with great care and asceticism. Even when she was on the pinnacle of her musical career and the world showered respect on her, she remained unfazed—music continued to be the sole purpose of her life, everything else was auxiliary.

Sawai Gandharva was extremely affectionate towards his disciple. Not once did this great musician, a chaste Brahmin at that, treat his disciple with contempt. It is notable that many musicians of this era were able to transcend boundaries of caste through their art. He was a devout Brahmin, believed in elaborate puja and ritual, but that only gave him the power to bring more people into the fold of his warmth and affection. His relationship with his guru Abdul Karim Khan was also similar. This was true of Abdul Karim Khan as well.

All this was happening as if in a parallel world when India was reeling under the bane of untouchability, when the chasms between Hindus and Muslims were widening, and the Mahatma had made it the mission of his life. It's a matter of great curiosity and interest how these social evils never became major impediments in the artistic world. Religion and caste hierarchy did not become hurdles for learning. There are ever so many instances of Muslim gurus and Hindu students, upper-caste *shishya*s and lower-caste gurus. They lived together in the *gurukula* system, and carried out duties. Even a conservative Lingayat like Mallikarjun Mansur learnt from Muslim gurus like Manji Khan and Burji Khan and revered them deeply. A highly conservative Madhwa Brahmin, Pt. Ramarao Naik, was the disciple of Ustad Faiyaz Khan. The ustad not only took him under his wings and taught him the robust and complex Agra style, but, for the ten long years that Ramarao Naik lived with him, Faiyaz Khan cooked rice and pulses in a separate kitchen for his prized disciple. Kabir, who was born to Muslim parents, and was the disciple of a Hindu guru, had said, "I am at once the child of Allah and Ram." The world of music in the Indian subcontinent resonates with the words of Kabir, where we see great gurus and their disciples effortlessly transcend worldly boundaries.

Concerning the relationship between music and politics, William Weber, in *The Rise of Musical Classics in Eighteenth-century England*, says, "[M]usical life both had its own politics and was part of that larger world." It was not surprising that the deeply conservative society of Gangubai's time failed to reconcile with the rather democratic world of art. Even as many of these individuals were extremely faithful to their own allegiances—be they devout Brahmins, Muslims or Lingayats—that never took away their respect for other belief systems. They were not judgemental in their understanding of other faiths or practices.

For instance, Faiyaz Khan saab was staunchly religious. He strictly offered namaaz five times a day. Just as he was eager to reach his audience through his music, he also sought union with God. A devout Muslim, he took part in Hindu festivals like Holi, Deepawali and several others. In fact, the Partition affected him deeply. Many of his friends and relatives moved over to Pakistan, but Khan saab refused to leave the country. Those close to Khan saab have recalled the extent to which he was influenced by Hindu culture, so much so that it was unthinkable for him to move to Pakistan. In fact, from his compositions one can hardly tell they are creations of a Muslim composer.

It is not necessary that musical traditions map on to social traditions. Tradition is not static, but evolves with individual redefinitions. Gangubai's adherence to her guru's music was testimony to her implicit faith in the musical tradition. However, her persona also emerged from her negotiations with social traditions. Gangubai became a prominent symbol of syncretism—

she worshipped her own private god, Mylaralinga, but also transcended it to enter the secular domain of art.

Baba Allauddin Khan saab, the maestro of Maihar, was not different either. He believed that oneness with God could be achieved only when the human being surrendered himself to the creative faculties. Baba was a devout Muslim, but his *sur sadhana* had brought him extremely close to Hindu gods as well. For someone as spiritual as he was, it was difficult to paint his notes with colours of caste. This extraordinary musician, who named his daughter Annapurna after the Hindu goddess, said that he experienced oneness with God only through his music. When Baba fell very ill, the doctors suggested that he be shifted to the hospital for treatment. Baba refused. He was a great devotee of Ma Sharada, and insisted that he die at her feet, and not in a hospital.

Tradition is replete with contradictory forces. In order to understand it, one must delve into its paradoxes. For instance, Pt. Ramarao Naik, who studied under the large-hearted maestro Ustad Faiyaz Khan, was extremely conservative, almost dogmatic. He was willing to learn music under a Muslim maestro, but was a fanatic casteist when it came to accepting students. How does one understand these idiosyncrasies? How was it that some artistes were able to transcend social boundaries through their art, while some couldn't? It remains a mystery why Sawai Gandharva refused to teach Mallikarjun Mansur. It couldn't have been the caste question—Sawai Gandharva had place for everyone. Could it perchance have been the dominance of the Lingayat caste in North Karnataka that prejudiced his views? Perhaps not. Sawai Gandharva had Lingayat students too.

The secular space of art emerged from the artiste's personal relationship to his religion. Even with private gods and very private practices of worship, the artiste was able to create a cosmos of his own where all gods coexisted under the shade of art. It was here that social evils had, perhaps, made peace with tradition. If tradition manifested itself differently in different geographical locations and contexts, the individual was entirely responsible for these variations.

* * *

Gangubai offered Sawai Gandharva a *gurudakshina* of Rs 1,001. It was a big sum in those days, but to have him as guru was priceless. She had put together those thousand rupees with enormous difficulty. "Money is transient, but a good disciple lives on," Sawai Gandharva had remarked to her with his characteristic generosity.

Guruji was a taskmaster. He wouldn't settle for anything less than perfect. For many months, he would leave her with a single melodic phrase for an entire day. While tending to household activities, he would pay attention to what his students were singing. If she made a mistake, he would storm into the room, demonstrate the correct manner, and ask Gangubai to repeat the phrase a few hundred times more. "*Pooriya Dhanashree* was my first raga. For three months, I have sung only *ga ga re sa ni pa, ni ni dha pa ma pa, ga ga re sa, ni dha pa ma ga re sa.* Then I would be bored to tears. *Sadhana* is lonely, as lonely as life itself. I wondered many a time if I even had a future in music. But I realized the value of all this rigorous intellectual hardship only in the later years."

The Kirana *gharana* emphasizes on unfolding the raga note by note. Each note is unravelled in its microtonal nuances, and the mystery of the raga is revealed only in its climactic moments. The music of the Kirana *gharana* emerges from a large canvas of silence—the singer meditates on each note leisurely, finally weaving a rich tapestry of intense melody. Sawai Gandharva never forgot to advise Gangubai about the economy of notes. "Be miserly with your *swara*s, don't unleash them all at once," he used to say.

The dry and dusty streets of Kundagol are embedded with stories. Its historic soil reverberates not just with music, but with stories about the people who made it remarkable. Gangubai and Bhimsen Joshi are the prized possessions of this modest, musical town. While Gangubai maintained very close ties with Kundagol till her very end, Bhimsen Joshi came only now and then. In the last two or three decades of his life he hardly visited Kundagol.

Bhimu's uncle was a station-master at the Gudigeri station close to Kundagol. In his itinerant search for a guru, he had landed at his uncle's house. In fact, it was Gangubai who took Bhimsen Joshi to Sawai Gandharva in the mid 1930s. As it is with most gurus, Bhimu also had to perform before Sawai Gandharva. After listening to him, there was no way Sawai Gandharva could refuse to take him on as his disciple. He came to stay with Sawai Gandharva in Kundagol and underwent training in the *gurukula* tradition. Gangubai was denied training in the *gurukula* mode because she was a woman. She also had a family to take care of. She would often say, "My gender was one impediment—I couldn't stay with my guru as a *shishya* does in the *guru-shishya parampara*—and my family was the other. It's all preordained. Nevertheless, it was my dharma to do *sangeeta tapasya.* I got what I deserved."

Bhimsen worked very hard on his music. He worked hard for the guru's household as well. After washing everyone's clothes, he would walk to the outskirts of Kundagol to fetch water from the well. It was the only well in the area, and he would make several trips with the pitchers on his shoulders. He made a minimum of twenty trips to the well every day, and all through the journey he would practise music. His shoulders would get sore and, many years later, the marks remained intact—reminders of his learning years. At night, he would go to his friends in the neighbourhood, borrow some oil, and give himself a massage. The next morning he would return to the same gruelling routine.

Once his chores were complete, his lessons would begin. Bhimu, as he was fondly called by all of Kundagol, would sit down for his *riyaz* at 10 p.m. and it would end only with sunrise. If one wondered what gave his music such astounding finesse and stability, the answer perhaps lies here. Very rarely did he sleep the nights.

If Bhimu and Gangu went on to become legends, they also owe it to the people of Kundagol who loved and nurtured these extremely talented musicians. They were mean and nasty to

Gangubai in the initial years, but as her music blossomed under the tutelage of a guru like Sawai Gandharva, they made amends. They came to love her as their own, lines of caste and social hierarchy gradually blurring.

A farmer of moderate means, who presently lives in the house of Sawai Gandharva, refused to sell it even for a big price. "If money was foremost in my life, I wouldn't have pledged all that I had to buy this house," he said during a visit.

In Harappa master's house there was a special place—a hole in the wall—outside the house. Here, every night before they went to sleep they kept a basket of food for dear Bhimu. The aspiring musician worked hard day and night. He would take his meals at Guruji's house, but there was always room for more. *Bhakri*, rice, *saaru* (*rasam*), brinjal curry—anything cooked that day would be kept for Bhimu. He religiously went to the attic, pulled out the cane basket, and helped himself to his second dinner before he sat down to practise. This was a ritual that went on for many years, for as long as Bhimu stayed in Kundagol. Now, Harappa master's house has been renovated, but "Bhimana Maadu" (Bhima's attic, as it came to be known) remains untouched. Gundappa Agnihotri, Narayana Bhat Birahatti, Kandakur—they all took turns to feed the promising Bhimu. His practice sessions were long, continuous and obsessive. They often led to the rupture of his nerves and his throat bled. But Bhimu had no time to worry over these things. His mind, body and soul were busy fathoming the mysteries of *Multani*, *Pooriya* and *Shuddha Kalyan*.

He often made up a pretext of accompanying Gangu to the railway station, and all along they discussed only music. "Guruji, it's getting dark and Gangu has to go alone to the station today. Don't you think I should walk with her?" Bhimu would propose. "Oh yes, of course. Knowing her, she will not ask. But you please go," Guruji would reply. The minute they started for the station, Bhimu would ask, "What did Guruji teach you today?" and plead, "Can you sing it for me till we reach the station …?" The two would talk music during the walk, the wait at the station, and until the train chugged off.

Though Bhimu wouldn't be a part of Gangu's lessons, he would move in and out of the house when they took place. He would linger a bit longer than necessary to listen to what she was singing. On one occasion, Sawai Gandharva was at his puja and Gangubai was practising a *palta.* "Gangu, you are singing it wrong," Bhimu interrupted the practice and began to sing the *palta* for her. Guruji, in a fit of rage, abandoned his puja, walked up to Bhimu and gave him a tight slap! "Who is the guru, you or me?" he thundered. That night as they walked to the station, Gangu had gently admonished her very dear *gurubandhu*, "You could have waited to tell me, couldn't you?" patting his back with affection. She was always so proud of him. His hard work and determination filled her heart. "He is a greater musician than I. In fact, he is unparalleled. I hope he gets the Bharat Ratna while I am around," she would often desire.

Once Sawai Gandharva and Bhimu got into a tiff. Guruji was so angry that he refused to teach Bhimu any further. "Out, this instant!" he had screamed and walked to his room in a huff. Poor Bhimu was stranded. Gangubai was heartbroken. She had to somehow resolve this. She ran to Harappa master, Dattopant and Keshavrao Patil to seek their advice on how to bring truce between guru and *shishya.* At no cost did she want Bhimu's lessons to come to an unceremonious end. All the four sat together and hatched a plan. Later, Bhimu was briefed about it as well. Bhimu was waiting just for this. He was very saddened by the entire episode and was restless to return into the fold of his guru.

On the appointed day, they put Bhimu into a room in Harappa master's house and asked him to practise. Sawai Gandharva had been invited. The guru settled down for a chat, completely unaware of the sequence of events to follow. In a little while, Sawai Gandharva heard strains of music, and he recognized Bhimu's voice. Initially, he looked uninterested. But he couldn't hold on to the pretence for long, he stopped talking. He was visibly moved and sat listening to Bhimu's music, intently. In an opportune moment, the four masterminds begged the maestro to take Bhimu back. "Please, please, Guruji … Take pity …" Gangu pleaded. "*Tappu hottege haakkolri*, please swallow his mistakes," she begged. How could he not relent?

Sawai Gandharva went across to the room where Bhimu was singing, and stood at the door. Bhimu looked at his guru and broke down. The next instant, Sawai Gandharva was holding his sobbing disciple close to his chest and consoling him. All was well, again.

Guruji had a quick temper, but it subsided quickly too. When he was unhappy with his other disciple Neelkanth Gadgoli, he said, "Enough, go back to Gadag." "He was inconsolable," Gangubai had recalled. "That whole day, all he did was practise. He didn't even stop for a drop of water. In the evening when Guruji returned home, he heard Gadgoli singing. He did not step inside the house, but sat outside for the next one hour." Then he entered, hung his coat and cap on the peg, and sat beside Gadgoli. "Don't go, stay," he patted his back and got up for a wash. "Poor Neelkanth … How much he had cried that day," Gangubai had said, with a tear in her eye. "He sobbed like his life had come to an end." Sawai Gandharva was an unusual guru. He treated his students like his children. His relation with them was full of ups and downs and differences. It was never casual or matter of fact. They had to measure up: talent was never a substitute for hard work.

Those days there was no electricity in Kundagol. Practice sessions in the evening had to take place under the light of the oil lamp. Sawai Gandharva would challenge his students, "Now let's see how powerful your *taan*s are?" and he would place the lantern at a certain distance. "If your *taan*s have power, then the light will be blown out," he would say. If music was difficult, *sadhana* was gruelling. Whether the light of the lantern went off or not was insignificant, it had to be the aim.

Apart from Bhimsen Joshi and Gangubai, there were other disciples like Venkatrao Ramdurg and Firoze Dastur. Firoze Dastur belonged to a wealthy Parsi family and could afford private tuitions. Sawai Gandharva went to Bombay, then, to give lessons to Firoze Dastur.

Sawai Gandharva was not the kind to tolerate any indiscipline. “I was so scared of him! To speak one line with him, I had to make up my mind for two days,” Gangubai would say with a shudder. Her fear would be so irrational that she would be mortified to even ask him the name of the raga she was being taught. Once, Sawai Gandharva was teaching her a new raga. She had been practising it for some time and had a fairly good grasp of it. Around this time All India Radio summoned her for a recording. She thought of presenting the raga she had been learning, but what was its name? Just the thought of asking her guru made her buckle under fear. Finally, Ramanna was given the task of asking Guruji.

It wasn’t easy for Ramanna either. He and Gangu planned how to go about the whole thing step by step. Sitting in front of Guruji, he pulled out a bunch of papers from his pocket. Just as they expected, Guruji asked: “What are all those papers in your pocket?” “Oh, these … AIR has sent a contract to Gangu. Do you think she should sing the new raga you are teaching her?” “Ragas don’t descend on you overnight. You have to be with them for a long period. They have to ferment,” saying this guruji started singing the raga. After listening to Guruji, Ramanna asked, “What is this raga called, Guruji?” Putting down his tanpura angrily, he uttered “*Suha, Suha*, *Suha*” three times in increasing intensity, and stomped out of the room in irritation. Quickly, Ramanna made a note of it!

Even after years of practice with Sawai Gandharva, her fears hadn’t diminished. Fakirappa Kundagol, who was also a practitioner of the Kirana *gharana,* ran a music school. For the annual function of the school, Sawai Gandharva’s recital would be followed by Gangubai’s. “I sat there with the tanpura, my legs shivering and my body breaking into a sweat. Much as I tried, my voice just wouldn’t come out of my throat. After a few embarrassing moments, I ran out of the stage, with tears flowing down my cheeks.” Guruji did not make any comments on that day, but later he would tease her recalling the incident.

It took many, many years before Gangubai earned the confidence of her Guruji. Each time she came back from a recording he would ask Ramanna, "How did she sing?" Ramanna would say, "She was good," and immediately Guruji would ask, "What do you mean by good? Please explain." He was not the kind who would let someone go easily. During one such "review meeting", Ramanna told Guruji that the audience had made a request for *Maru Bihag* and Gangu refused to sing it since she had not been taught the raga. The next thing Guruji did was to summon Gangubai. He sat down to teach her *Maru Bihag*. The next three days he was obsessed with it. On the fourth day, when she turned up at his house, he asked her to sing the raga, and went about doing his work. She waited and waited, hoping that he would come, sit before her, guide her—but that was not going to happen. Morning passed into afternoon, and afternoon into evening. Guruji had finished his morning activities, eaten lunch, and completed his afternoon siesta. His cup of piping hot tea soon arrived, and yet he did not come up to Gangu. She waited tense and restless, almost ready to cry. On seeing her condition, Guruji's wife went up to him and said, "Why don't you go? The poor girl is nervous."

"She is singing so well, she doesn't need my help," he had remarked. "These are things I can never forget," Gangubai would remember with amazing clarity. She would pull her *pallu* to wipe her tears and say, "He was a true student of music. Even when he had students the whole day, he would wake up at 3.30 in the morning for his *riyaz.* If he had some free time during any part of the day, he would sit down to practise. That was his level of dedication." In her autobiography, Gangubai notes, "He would practise different aspects of the *swara*, *alaap*, *ghasit*, *murkhi*, *khatka* and *raga.* This continued till he was completely satisfied with himself. At times, he practised only *vilambit* or the changeover from *kharaj vilambit* to madhya *shadja* for the whole day." Sawai Gandharva believed in unending *sadhana.* Every day, he chased a new challenge and struggled to better himself.

Guruji spoke little and hardly praised his disciples. All his conversations were mostly about music. Whenever Gangubai went to Bombay for her AIR recordings, Sawai Gandharva would either be there for a concert or for Firoze Dastur's lessons. He would invariably have listened to her on the radio. "If Guruji had a quarrel with what I sang, he would never hesitate to tell me what was wrong. It had to be settled then and there, at that very instant. After unburdening himself, he would be fine. If he liked my singing, he would say, 'Okay Gangu, get up, let's go have a cup of hot, flavoured milk.' He would summon the Victoria, a horse-drawn carriage, and drive to a particular shop in Kalbadevi. The milk would be spiked with saffron, almonds and cardamom, and tasted divine! What a treat that used to be!"

Nāda nadī—the river of resonances

The body a divine veena
Each nerve a string
Throbbing dawn to dusk, the breath is the song
Strum it you proficient
Mother, I have surrendered myself
into thine hands, let the music of the soul emerge*

— Da. Ra. Bendre

The oneness of thought and emotion a Bhakti poet achieves in his poetry is not drastically different from what a folk singer aspires to in his song. In both their journeys, abstractions get translated into tangible experiences. The routes, however, are different. The folk singer, with his sensibilities firmly rooted in the soil, suggests the philosophical dimension of human existence, whereas the Bhakti poet demythologizes the divine and spiritual, transporting them back into the everydayness of human life.

Dattatreya Ramachandra Bendre, the mystic poet of Kannada, stitched together word, sound and philosophical thought with remarkable felicity, bringing together the best of Bhakti and the folk. His poetry captures the climate of creative life in Hubli and Dharwad during the early twentieth century. One can discern his influence on the people who formed the artistic crust of the region. In Bendre's poetry, his profound connection with music is evident. He saw the interconnected nature of all things, a notion he may

* The excerpts from the poems of Bendre and Basavanna are translated by the author.

have derived from music. He is also a master at transforming philosophical abstraction into vibrant emotion.

Bendre was of the belief that, for a poet, choosing the right word and, for the musician, hitting the right musical note or holding the *jeeva swara* were never easy tasks. These resulted from a deep churning of the soul, he maintained. In his poem "Naadaleele", which literally means "the mystery of resonance", Bendre keeps expanding the meaning of the most crucial word *naada. Naada* at once means sound, resonance, reverberation, and also knead. In the climactic moments of the poem, he brilliantly yokes tradition with the present. Using the image of the tree, he says that the height of the tree is determined by the depth of its roots—in other words, the present must live with a consciousness of the past. Bendre's practice of poetry and music captures the climate of creative life in Hubli and Dharwad during the early twentieth century. His influence on the artistic community there was striking as well. The convergence of emotion and intellect in Gangubai was akin to the synthesis of the rich tradition of Bhakti and folk in Bendre. Never privileging one over the other, she was wary of her music becoming a pure intellectual quest. That's perhaps why she never differentiated between the classical genre and the devotional. "Everything that my guru has taught me is devotional, so I have never found the need to sing a *devaranama*," she would say. The sum total of all these resonances, within and without, made up the character of her music.

In spite of having a keen intellect, Gangubai's meagre school education prevented her from articulating her own thoughts about her art. But, on watching her closely, you knew she would answer these questions in the time to come. She could not build the discourses that the poet Bendre or the musician Kumar Gandharva could build around their practices. She was incapable of holding forth on her musicology, unlike her fairly articulate contemporaries. But if this leads us to underestimate her intelligence it is folly. She drew attention to herself only through her music.

* * *

Bendre was not only a great poet but also a profound thinker. He argued that the creative processes of the writer and the musician are similar. Due to his understanding of music, and the manner in which he could integrate the philosophy of music with that of literature, he aligned himself with most musicians of his time in Dharwad. He was highly revered by people, and was close to legendary musicians such as Mallikarjun Mansur, Bhimsen Joshi, Kumar Gandharva, Basavaraj Rajguru, Gangubai Hangal, Sawai Gandharva and Shankar Dikshit Jatanjali. Despite his knowledge of classical texts he never lost sight of the experiential dimension of an individual's life. In fact, like the twelfth-century radical Bhakti poet Basavanna, the Sadhanakeri bard Bendre too makes a case for *bhaava* over *buddhi,* for feeling over "intellect".

If Basavanna said:

> I know not the balance of rhythm and measure
> I know not the arithmetic of the beat structure
>
> …
>
> O Lord Koodalasangama, without tainting you,
> I shall sing this song of my desire

One finds similar feelings in Bendre's poem "Sakhigeeta":

> When the word becomes one with the beat
> Does one count the stresses in each cycle?
> When the resonance of love soaks the senses
> Does one ask, which raga is this?

While sticking to the classical framework, Bendre believed in a certain abandon: the ability to shed oneself in the passionate pursuit of higher, sublime things. In a way, the highly original Kumar Gandharva came close to Bendre's thinking. In the creative process, the ideational had to be found in the experiential. It was not something that happened in the mind alone, it had a physical location. Bendre emphatically believed that when music or literature became mere intellectual quests, they were bound to fail.

Sitting before a fish tank, admiring the lyrical, buoyant movement of the fish, Kumar Gandharva had said in admiration: "Wish one could achieve this movement with the *swara*s!" On another occasion, while delineating a raga, two *swara*s that did not belong to the raga crept into it. Critics made a hue and cry: "How could you do this?" Kumar Gandharva had quietly replied: "As I was singing, these two notes came up to me and pleaded to be given a chance. So I took them in."

Bendre's poetry was similar and so were his speeches. He would go off in what seemed like completely disconnected directions, like the fish in the tank, but what emerged finally was a single, comprehensive picture. Bendre's writing and speech had the structure of music. With an overarching synergy, it came packed with the most unanticipated sparks.

From the song of the roaming *budibudike dasayya*—the itinerant alms seeker who went from house to house singing devotional verses in earthy, folk style—to chaste classical music, Bendre's canvas was large. At times, he stood at the gate listening to the music in street cries, to the flower seller, the vegetable vendor, and so on. Both literature (the word, sound and meaning) and music, were *upaasane* (worship) for him.

* * *

Bendre never refused an invitation to a concert. Even when he was in the middle of his writing, he attended every concert that took place in Hubli–Dharwad. Musicians took it as a blessing to have Bendre in the audience, because his nuanced understanding often provided them a new perspective. He never left a concert midway and not even once did he complain that music disturbed his creative equilibrium. On the contrary, he often said that it provided nourishment to his thoughts, an impetus to his creative moorings. One artistic pursuit never existed outside the other.

Bendre and his opinions were so valued that the mighty often came knocking at his door. Bhimsen Joshi—who referred to Bendre as *daivamsha sambhootaru*, an embodiment of godliness—was singing in Dharwad, and Bendre was, of course, there to listen to him. It was a concert that just did not work out for Joshi. Many in the audience left half way, but Bendre sat through the entire concert. However, having become pensive by the end of the concert, he left without talking to Joshi.

At around 2.30 a.m., there was a furious knock on Bendre's door. The poet accompanied by his son Vaman anxiously rushed to the door, and was surprised to see a distraught Bhimsen Joshi. "I am very disturbed," he said, putting his trembling hands into Bendre's. "My nagging domestic problems and vices got the better of me today. I am determined to come and sing for the *sabha* again at my own expense. Why did I fail? Somehow, I felt the raga denied me entry, please explain," he pleaded, standing at the doorstep.

Bendre put his hand comfortingly around Joshi and led him inside. Nothing could comfort him. It seemed like an endless night. Bendre promised to explain—but through a poem. Bendre's poem "Yeru" had begun to take shape during the concert itself.

Raga eridante yeru—"Rise as the raga does"—Bendre recited with impact from the poem. Making the self unimportant is crucial in the creative process. It is a continual surrender to something that is more valuable. The artistic process, as T.S. Eliot said, "is a continual extinction of personality."

What if you swing to the left, or to the right?
It's the path all the same

Bendre adds, putting his entire approach to Indian music in perspective. Modern Indian classical music, which came into being in his generation, never had a definite aesthetic goal. Knowing this, he says,

Hold on to the root, rise,
Passion and pattern hand in hand

Bendre, like Ananda Coomaraswamy, holds that in Indian creative art, the artiste is always secondary.

Journey to the land
that knows the plight of the singer …

For Bendre, it was the process not the end result that mattered. Surrender was central to the creative process, and hence occasional failures hardly mattered to him.

Joshi, on reading the poem, wept. He told Bendre, "The poem is in my prayer book. I read it every day. The day I sing it will be the last day of my life."

Bendre left a deep impact on everyone he met. He even wrote a poem on the legendary Jaipur maestro Mallikarjun Mansur, calling him the soul-stealer—*Mana Sooregonda Manasura.* For Gangubai, he was many things rolled into one. He had great affection for her, and knew that much of what he believed and practised formed the unsaid in her.

Gangubai knew Bendre as early as 1919. In fact, he lived in the same locality as she and her mother: Kamanakatte. When she was a student of the Rashtreeya Vidyalaya in Dharwad, a school started by the Kannada writer Alur Venkata Rao, Bendre taught there. That's where he became Bendre Master, and remained so for the rest of his life. Gangubai remembered him not only as a teacher who was the personification of poetry but also as a person of immense warmth. He treated his students like friends. This meant a lot to the little Gangu who was terrified of school. This relationship with Bendre that started in 1919, continued till the end.

Throughout her life, Gangubai valued the companionship and opinion of two people—Bendre and the writer N.K. Kulkarni. They were her friends, guides and philosophers, so much so that, in the early years, whenever she practised a new raga, she would perfect it in the presence of Bendre and N.K. Whenever she had a concert in Hubli or Dharwad she would send word for them, and they would promptly turn up. She always remembered them with a deep sense of gratitude.

Though Gangubai had abstained from singing any form of music other than the *khayal* after the initial years, Bendre, in a manner of supporting her decision, had told her: "Let Krishna sing *dasara pada*, not you." He felt that her voice merged into the resonance of sound, and hence lost the emotion required to sing Bhakti music. "There is an intimate relationship between *bhava* and *naada*. I feel, only Krishna should sing the lighter forms," Bendre had explained one evening. This reinforced her stand. However, her resolve to not sing devotional compositions was shaped by very different reasons.

When Gangubai left for a concert tour of America in 1979, hundreds gathered at the Dharwad railway station to see her off. She was hoping Bendre would come too. It was almost time for departure, and when she had lost hope of seeing Bendre and receiving his good wishes, she saw him hurrying up the platform, in his characteristic Chinese-collared black coat and black cap. Wishing Gangubai and her daughter Krishna, he had gently placed something in Gangubai's hands—a monkey cap. "You'll need it, it's a cold country," he had said. He also gave her a copy of his latest collection of poems. It was on that day, just as the train was chugging out of the Dharwad station and hundreds of local admirers stood waving on the platform, that Bendre famously said: "Gangubai's song touches the skies and Krishna's touches the heart." Armoured with these heartfelt wishes, Gangubai left, but only after touching his feet. "Such friendships are hard to find," she would remember later, unable to say more.

In the Dharwad cultural scene, the figure of Bendre was central to most serious artistes. When he was literary advisor to All India Radio, Dharwad, he came to meet many musicians. In those days, Bendre wrote a musical called *Dhanyavrundavana.* Mallikarjun Mansur, Basavaraj Mansur, Gangubai Hangal and Basavaraj Rajguru sang for it. Bendre gave each of these singers a free hand

and asked them to utilize the Hindustani classical style. Of course, he had an extended session with them on the title and its meaning, and also explained to them what he expected out of it musically.

N.K., Gangubai's very dear friend, also the narrator of her autobiography *Nanna Badukina Haadu* (The Song of My Life), in his foreword to a monograph on the poet, speaks of how Bendre would turn up at his house, a bag slung over his shoulder, with many books. "He would say I'm going around seeking alms of *samvaada,* dialogue," recalls N.K. who used to have extensive discussions with the poet. "What I have gained intellectually is hard to put in words," N.K. said. Like N.K., Gangubai and a whole host of creative minds benefited immensely from him.

Bendre believed in a multidisciplinary approach to art and in creative exchange. He knew that his creative and philosophical pursuits did not end in his own self: the self only served as the starting point.

For Gangubai, Bendre was also a major source of spiritual strength. Her life was so full of troubles, her music so replete with dilemmas in the initial years that Bendre and his philosophy served to strengthen her moral fibre. Since she built a world of stories from her life and lived there, anyone who entered into a conversation with her also came to inhabit that world. But as Bendre believed, the song did not merely encompass *aahata*—the heard resonances—but also the *anaahata*—the unheard resonances. Gangubai's life and music are like the *aahata naada* (heard resonances) that emerge from and also melt into unheard resonances. If her stock stories form the "heard" of her life and music, the unarticulated forms the "unheard" of her life. According to Indian musicology, all the twenty-two pitches of music dwell in the *anaahata* and a seeker seeks his answers in the realm of unheard resonances. This, as Bendre knew, was not easy.

Must dig into the inner recesses
Must uncover the spiritual
Must have the Guru's boundless guidance

We need resonance, knead resonance
Till the summit is attained, knead resonance

Gangubai abstained from flashy presentations. Her music was shorn of dazzling artistry. It was a silent, serious pursuit. In fact, while she drew from the *anaahata* to strengthen her music, she drowned much of what she did not want to say into the *anaahata* as well. Did Bendre write the following lines with her in mind? Or does one find the resonances of Bendre's poetry in Gangubai's artistry?

Let my fate be, the song alone is my offering
O' connoisseur
If your crystal sugar like heart melts,
shower only its sweetness on me ....

Guru bina kaise guṇ gāve ...

When Sawai Gandharva came to live in Hubli, Gangubai would be thrilled to be part of his *riyaz* sessions. She would listen to him unfold the notes, and each utterance would sound spectacularly different from the earlier one. She once said: "The way he elaborated on the 'miyal' was special. He was always bursting with ideas. After listening to his *riyaz* I would be inspired to undertake rigorous practices, surrendering completely to the pursuit of music." Sawai Gandharva was a near perfect teacher and musician. To master the *swara* and flesh out its microtonal nuances, one had to follow a military regimen. By paying attention to accuracy, timing and synchronization, one had to engage in blind repetition, without wearing oneself out. Sawai Gandharva did all this with great austerity, as if it were a penance.

In the early forties, Sawai Gandharva had a paralytic stroke, and decided to move to Pune to stay with his daughter. When he returned to Hubli after his treatment, Gangubai insisted that he should stay with her. Her house was modest, she had a large family, the going was difficult—but this would not deter her. Sawai Gandharva and his wife came to stay with her. She looked after them with utmost care and devotion. She never let her difficulties affect them. He continued to be treated for his illness for the next three years.

Gangubai had now begun to receive offers for programmes, including those for All India Radio. When she would sit to practise, Sawai Gandharva would become emotional. He would shed silent tears, being deeply touched by his disciple's music. He felt grateful for her loving care. There were times when, unable to control his emotions, he would slowly walk up to her and say: "There is so much more that I need to teach you. Bring the tanpura." Gangubai was worried that this would disturb his delicate health. But Sawai Gandharva would be in no mood to listen to her words. "He would weakly walk up to me and start teaching me a new raga. How many times he has done this!" she said forlornly, looking at the room in which he had stayed. Once, he even told her, "I took Rs 1,000 from you during the *Ganda Bandhan*. You paid me a monthly fee of Rs 40. I took too much from you—I haven't taught you enough in return, have I?" Gangubai would hear no more. "What I have received from you is priceless. Please, Guruji," she would implore him to stop. "I feel I haven't given you all the music I know. My health is playing truant and it makes me feel miserable," he would brood.

A lot was happening in Gangubai's career as a musician. She was travelling, meeting fellow musicians, and making new friendships which would become lasting relationships in her life. During her first concert in 1933 at the Suburban Magic Circle in Bombay she was noticed by HMV. They signed her for a series of rpm recordings. When she began singing for All India Radio, Bombay, in 1936, it wasn't yet a government body. Only years later would it become a government enterprise. Gangubai is among the few musicians of this country who mark the evolution of this mega institution.

In 1943, she was invited to perform at the Gaya Music Conference. Ustad Bade Ghulam Ali Khan, Ustad Faiyaz Khan, and many other legendary musicians were performing there as well. Gangubai was excited about performing amidst such stalwarts. But, sadly, when her turn came, she only got fifteen minutes. She was so disappointed that she could not hide it: sitting in a corner she put her head down and tears rolled down her cheeks. The shehnai maestro, Bismillah Khan, went up to her and consoled her. "Don't think fifteen minutes is little time. You can make a big impact with it. Get up, wipe your tears and go now." She sang a vibrant Raga *Basant*, and the audience found this young newcomer extremely engaging. But the response of the audience hardly elevated Gangubai's spirits. The following day a party was thrown by the organizers, and Gangubai was requested to sing. After the previous day's experience she had felt so slighted, that she refused to sing. Ustad Bade Ghulam Ali Khan saab, who was present, understood the agony of this young lady. He went up to her and said, "You must sing. If you do, I too will." Moved by his gesture, she agreed. That evening when she sang *Shuddha Kalyan* there was no one to stop her. Her elaborate presentation won her enormous love and affection from musicians and connoisseurs.

The other incident that she often remembered was how her diminutive stature and plain looks often caused her trouble. Jaddan Bai, Nargis's mother, had recommended her for the Music Conference in Calcutta. But the organizers, on seeing her, weren't sure of her calibre. "You will have to rehearse before the committee," they told her categorically. Gangubai was shaken. The doyen of Rampur-Sahaswan *gharana*, Ustad Nisar Hussain Khan felt sad for her. He told her how he too had to accept such treatment from the organizers when he was invited for his first performance. "Look at it this way: it will be good for you and your accompanists to comprehend each other's music. That was how I looked at it. Go ahead, everything will be fine," he instilled confidence in her.

Calcutta holds many memories for Gangubai—happy and sad. K.L. Saigal, Kanan Bala and Pahadi Sanyal would always turn up for a concert by her. Once, she sang the *cheez* made famous by Abdul Karim Khan—*Piya Bina Naahin Avat Chain*—and the audience showered her with applause. The king of Tripura honoured her with a gold medal. After the performance, Gangubai went to a corner of the stage and wept remembering her mother. Saigal, who just could not go away without congratulating the young musician, came backstage and put his hand on her shoulder. Aghast at this unexpected touch, she turned around angrily and discovered it was none other than the man of stentorian voice—Saigal. Sheepishly, she accepted his compliments: *Bahut surila* (Amazing sweetness)!

In her late thirties, Gangubai suddenly began to have problems with her throat. For a while she ignored it. But then, during her concert tours this disturbed her: it would interrupt her singing, and she needed a constant supply of hot water. Her doctor Joshi diagnosed her condition as tonsillitis, and suggested surgery. She was warned, however, that in the worst case she could lose her voice for good. She did not have a choice, she had to take the plunge. "They passed an electric current through my throat and burnt that extra flesh. After that, the texture of my voice changed completely. It started sounding like a male voice. The people who had heard my voice earlier could barely recognize it later. It was thin and sharp, much like that of Krishna's. Anyway, it did not bother me much, because I had not lost the ability to sing."

If Abdul Karim Khan was accepted with his melodious, womanly voice texture, why should a male voice be an obstacle for Gangubai? But things were not as simple as that. She was laughed at and ridiculed for the androgynous nature of her voice. It had taken away the fluidity of her earlier voice texture, but nevertheless her music had been bestowed with a rare resonance in exchange. In fact, not undermining the profundity and sincerity of her music, Bendre had once said, "Probably a cursed Gandharva resides in her throat." This was at once a comment about her exalted music and the nature of her voice. But a comment about the maleness of her voice was the last of her worries. Her understanding of the "voice" was much deeper.

Remembering the following incident gave her cause for amusement very often: she was broadcasting from AIR, Delhi. She was staying with a friend on that trip, and had asked her friend's daughter to listen to her as she was going live. Upon returning from the performance, Gangubai asked the young girl if she enjoyed her music, and pat came the reply: "Aunty, I switched on the radio exactly on time. But it was some man singing and not you, so I switched it off." For the next few minutes Gangubai laughed uncontrollably, before she finally told the girl, "That man was me!" Voice was only a medium for her. She also had this unusual ability to laugh at herself.

She even acted in a Marathi film, *Vijayache Lagna.* There was a music concert in the film, and Gangubai had to play the musician. So she sang before the camera. This fifteen-minute tryst with the camera was her first and last.

What Gangubai considered a rare honour was singing at the sixtieth-birthday celebrations of her guru, Sawai Gandharva, in 1946, which took place at the Sawai Gandharva Hall in Hubli. She shared the stage with her Guruji. This time, singing with her guru did not cause in her the fear that she had felt previously. It was an offering to a person who was her life. She did it with unmatched devotion and grace. Till her last moments, there was never a time when she did not remember him. "She was large-hearted. She showered love on everybody. But there were two people who truly mattered to her the most: her mother and her guru. The others always gained by her affection. But in spirit, she always lived in the warmth of these two people," her grandson Manoj Hangal often remarked.

Sawai Gandharva moved back to Pune after having spent three years under Gangubai's care. His illness had forced him to cast off his phenomenal musical persona, leaving him in great anguish. His contemporaries recall that he would occasionally weep and lament the fact that he could no longer sing. The suffering he went through was immeasurable. Caught between his desire to sing and a body that would just not cope, Sawai Gandharva's health was on a steady decline. In 1952, on 12 September, Sawai Gandharva breathed his last.

Gangubai had barely recovered from her mother's departure, and here her guru, too, was gone. She felt uprooted. The man who stood by her during the most difficult times, who gave her emotional support after her mother's death, was gone. Gangubai found it extremely difficult to come to terms with it. Ten years of his suffering had come to an end, but it was also the end of an era: a direct disciple of the founder of the Kirana *gharana*, Abdul Karim Khan saab, was no more.

All over Maharashtra there was a deep sense of loss. Vamanrao Deshpande, a renowned musicologist, paid a tribute to him from All India Radio, Bombay. It was broadcast on the very same day—

12 September. An excerpt from the moving tribute, originally in Marathi, reads like this:

> I deeply regret that Rambhau Kundagolkar, who earned the title Sawai Gandharva, left the world this morning at 5.30 a.m. He was 68 years of age. He spent the last decade in great physical pain. The last ten years of his life were very difficult, his illness had left him tired. Since he was paralysed, doctors had advised him not to sing. In the recent years, his failing health had shaken him so much that he too feared singing, so much so that he would not even hum. For an artiste of such remarkable calibre, who was passionately with music all his life, what else could he do but sit before his tanpuras and weep, cursing cruel fate, which he often did!
>
> I visited him once in a while and each time we met, he said: "Can a musician be struck with greater tragedy?" He had to satisfy himself by simply talking about music.
>
> Rambhau Kundagolkar had captured the hearts of thousands of music lovers and his music to this day rings in their ears. If you met a musician or a connoisseur the conversation would invariably turn towards Rambhau. Then it would slowly turn towards his ill health and unfailingly they would express their anxiety.
>
> I was fortunate to have heard him many a times. The last time I got to hear him was at his 60th birthday celebrations that took place in Pune. That day he sang raga Jogiya, *Hari ka bhed na paayo* in jhaptaal for ten minutes. He was in no position to sing. But then when people were honouring him how could he go away without singing for them? He felt he owed it to them and the audience was mesmerised by the manner in which he had packed in so many shades of his music despite his physical condition. The *cheez* was rendered with force, brilliant understanding of rhythm, and chiselled *taan*s, *vilambit*, everything was just so perfect. It was like a model of perfect singing.
>
> It's not easy to sing the Abdul Karim Khan *bani.* Firstly, you have to train your voice in a particular way, so that it produces emotions befitting Abdul Karim Khan's school. In spite of his voice problems, he worked tirelessly to soften all the rough edges so that he could produce the desired effect.
>
> He listened to all his contemporaries and desired to bring in the finer aspects of all their music into his own. For instance, Bhaskhar Bua, whom he admired a great deal, formed a large part of his music. His style in *natyasangeet* was unique and inimitable. Though he was the disciple of a great maestro, he strived hard to have an identity and style that was his own. If he had chosen not

to be a mere imitator of Khan sahib or not just his mirror image, it was only because he was a true student of music.

When a musician is famous in the real sense of the word, it means his music transcends the boundaries of a *gharana* and brings all musicians into the fold of his music. Rambhau was one such. His devotion for his guru was exemplary. I remember a famous artiste once went to him for a photograph—he wanted to hang it in his music school. Rambhau had asked him: 'Tell me, have you put up my guruji's picture in your music school? Please get his picture first, later you can ask me for mine.'

Rambhau's disciples weren't too many but he produced stalwarts. If the illness had not taken away those ten precious years from his life, he would have trained a couple more. Gangubai Hangal, Bhimsen Joshi, Master Krishna Rao, Feroz Dastur, Kagalkar Bua, Dr Deshpande, Indirabai Khadilkar and others. With the death of Sawai Gandharva an entire generation of legendary musicians have come to an end. The path ahead is now filled with darkness.

This ended a major chapter in Gangubai's life as well. After her mother she had looked to her guru for support and, now that he too had gone, Gangubai felt orphaned.

* * *

Life had to go on nevertheless. Her children were growing up and the needs of her family were growing too. From carrying firewood, to cooking, cleaning and assisting her aunts, to practising and performing—life had to go on. There was no escape. "We used to have a lot of guests all the time. We were a huge household, you see … nearly twenty of us at home. And when fellow musicians came home I couldn't help much with cooking. I had two aunts—wives of my maternal uncles—who cooked, while I served. When I went into the kitchen to get the dishes, they would whisper to me with a quiet eagerness, 'What do the guests look like?' I would want them to come out, but shy that they were, they would even refuse to stand behind the door and peep. When they sensed that the guests were ready to leave, they would run to the backyard to catch a glimpse before they got into the tonga."

Soon after Guruji's death Gangubai got a contract from AIR Delhi for her first national musical programme. She was in no mood for this, and was almost on the verge of declining the contract. But her family and well-wishers convinced her to accept it. Overpowered by reminiscences of her long and loving association with Sawai Gandharva, Gangubai made a poignant presentation, a tribute to her guru. Much later, she remembered, "It felt as if Guruji's music was flowing in my veins. Even now, I often have the illusion that he is teaching me. AIR received many letters in praise of my programme. Even though Ramanna had been too ill to accompany me that day, he had sent me a telegram from Hubli which said: 'Today, you sounded exactly like Guruji.' What a life …" she would trail off.

"I had to wake up early and practise for a couple of hours, before my household duties took over. Then in the evening, on days when I was in Hubli, we would practise for an hour or two." Gangubai's method of practice was exactly like her guru's. It involved a lot of repetition and was highly monotonous. The phrases and *swara*s deployed in a particular raga would be studied. This is because Sawai Gandharva would always emphasize upon the manner in which a raga had to be presented. The opening phrase should have the right placement of *swara*s, and should immediately reveal to the listener the raga the musician is singing. Gangubai would say that this method took her a long way. Even when she dealt with a new raga, she had an instinctive grasp of its notes. She often quoted Ustad Karim Khan saying to Pt. Sawai Gandharva that he would teach only three ragas—a morning raga, an evening melody and a night raga. Apparently Karim Khan saab would say that, while he would teach his students Todi, Pooriya and Multani, it was up to them to deal with the other ragas. "The way he trained us was remarkable. It has kept me in good stead until now. I haven't been able to do *riyaz* for many years now, but I have forgotten nothing," she said.

At this time, Akashvani was spreading its reach. In 1950, AIR Dharwad was launched, and it was closely followed by Nagpur and Pune. Most stations would invite Gangubai for the inaugural performance. She loved singing for AIR, for she knew that no matter which part of the country she sang in, people back in Hubli would listen to her. AIR took these artistes across the length and breadth of the country and made them household names. Public concerts were still not in vogue. AIR was the most powerful medium for musicians. Occasionally, rich patrons invited these artistes home for a private concert, but this was the fortune only of a select audience. It didn't make too much economic sense to sing for AIR. "I sang for the inauguration of AIR Bombay. They gave me Rs 50. The train fare from Hubli to Pune was Rs 8.50, and from there the broad gauge train to Bombay cost a rupee and two annas. So, for Ramanna and me, journeying up and down would cost Rs 40. In effect, we could save Rs 10. The money was not much, but the biggest incentive was that my Hubli people could listen to me."

Since the AIR station in Bombay had been inaugurated about fifteen years ahead of the other stations, music *sabha*s invariably tied her AIR recordings up with public concerts when Gangubai visited Bombay. This is how they would save on her travel expenditure. "There were four music groups in Bombay—Arts Circle, Indian Music Circle, Bombay Music Circle, and Arts Society. They would all book me together. In Maharashtra, Ganesh Chaturthi was a big affair. Huge *pandal*s would be erected in Chunnam Lane and Topiwala Lane. I was invited to sing every season, due to which I never got to stay home for the festival. On these trips I saw Tilak and Gokhale, but never got to talk to them," she had recalled. What mattered to Gangubai was the presence of great musicians at her concert: "Manji Khan, Bhurji Khan, Saraswati Bai Narvekar, Hirabai Badodekar—everyone would be present, and in the first row. I would be extremely nervous, despite their inspiring presence. Such a thing is unthinkable now. Once, after the concert, Hirabai invited me for lunch the next day. After lunch, her mother Tarabai said, 'Why don't you stay back in Bombay. It will be good for your career. You can start by accepting the programmes that Champu Tai refuses.' It had infuriated me so much. Tarabai was capable of sarcasm, but Hirabai was a gem. Those were great times despite all the difficulties. Very often, I would be singing in one *pandal* and, close by, in another, Hirabai would be singing."

Even though radio had firmly established itself in India, not too many people could afford a radio. Since gramophones were still around in the music market, most hotels and shops played them. Gangubai would often speak of The Grand Hotel in Dharwad, which had a good collection of gramophone records and played them through the day. "They had recordings by Karim Khan saab, my guru Sawai Gandharva and me. So while you enjoyed your dosa, you even got to listen to music," she would say chuckling.

Koregaonkar, a harmonium player who had a shop in Durgada Bail, was another informed listener. His stock of records was so good that people loved visiting his store. He himself had been recorded by HMV. The ambience of his shop of musical instruments was charged when he played records through the day. Music lovers found this inviting.

"Those days everything was a unique experience: I was learning every moment. Gramophone recordings would take precisely three minutes and twenty seconds. In the absence of timers, the recording officers would indicate the end of every minute with their fingers. Of course, All India Radio had the red light. That would come up," she reminisces. When the blind, visionary musician Panchakshara Gawai recorded for gramophone companies, the recording officer would apparently sit behind him, his hand wrapped in cloth, and, at the end of every minute, place his finger on the wrist of the visionary to tell him how much time was left.

Before Partition Gangubai went to Pakistan on several occasions. Even later, she performed from AIR Lahore at least six times and once from Karachi. Once Mr Bokhari, the director of AIR Bombay, persuaded her to perform from Peshawar. She refused because she was wary about travelling through the Khyber Pass. But Bokhari's persistence did rope her into chain-booking performances in both Lahore and Peshawar. After performing in Lahore, she was sent to Peshawar by car. After travelling for three days, Gangubai was exhausted. She decided to take a leisurely bath, she washed her hair and stood in the balcony for it to dry.

The hotel manager, who caught a glimpse of her from the street below, came running up and anxiously said, "Please get in, please get in." And once he had pushed her back within the four walls of the room, he said, "Women cannot stand in public in this country. We follow the Gosha." Gangubai never got over this. Whenever she spoke about the radio days, she would invariably narrate the incident. "See … the kinds of things they impose on women in the name of tradition. Imagine, me going around with a veil …" she would make light of the matter.

Later, in the post-Independence years, she was invited to perform at the Pakistan Utsav. She was conferred the Hafeez Ali Award for her contribution to Hindustani music. The citation of the award said that at a time when there weren't too many women in the profession, Gangubai popularized Hindustani music in the south against all odds. "You are an important bridge between north and south India."

After the initial years of trepidation and test, Gangubai participated in most music conferences. At a conference in Calcutta, Kesarbai Kerkar was supposed to sing after her. This suited her well—she did not want to sing after a senior musician like her. When Gangubai first met her on a train journey from Bombay to Delhi, Kesarbai was hostile. Gangubai had been disturbed by this. Only after the older musician had heard Gangubai a couple of times did she greet her cordially. On this occasion in Calcutta, Kesarbai requested to sing before her because she was ill, and could not wait for too long. No one had the courage to turn down Kesarbai's request, for she was the queen and always had the last word. Later, when Kesarbai was in the hospital, Gangubai with Ramanna and Narayan Rao Indorekar went to see her. She was on the verge of slipping into a coma, and couldn't open her eyes fully or speak. Gangubai went close to her and said "Bai, I'm Gangubai. I have come to see you." Rather incoherently and with a drawl, Kesarbai said: "Oh yes, haven't we sung together?" When Narayan Rao Indorekar announced himself, she said: "Have you brought your tabla?" She didn't survive for too long after that.

Gangubai's career slowly and steadily gathered momentum. She was making a place for herself in the world of classical music with her unique voice and aesthetic. Life, however, was never kind on her. In the face of difficulties, Gangubai gave herself to music with commitment.

Like fragrances taking flight on wayward wind

Gandhiji was integral to Gangubai's way of life. This attachment came from her childhood experiences, when the streets were charged with the energies of the freedom struggle, and from her own personal encounter with the struggle in the Belgaum Congress. She would say that there was always something soothing about his presence. Even though she grew up in the thick of the freedom struggle, she rarely spoke of it. It was not as if her world was isolated from what was happening outside, but she never seemed to have the language for it. Gangubai did not indulge in great rhetoric. She was, instead, more interested in right action.

Gangubai would speak of the meetings and speeches held in Durgadbail: "How they were charged with patriotic fervour! It would make my hair stand on end, and produce a strange churning in my belly …" Every morning people marched through the streets singing patriotic songs. A great sense of exhilaration filled the air. "I, too, would trail behind them for some distance and run back home."

Dharwad was tanked up with anti-British feelings like elsewhere in the country, and was also high on intellectual activity. R.S. Hukkeri dreamt of an integrated Karnataka and ran a journal called *United Karnataka.* G.B. Joshi, a writer, edited the literary journal *Jeevana.* Closer to the attainment of freedom, there was a journal called *Vishala Karnataka*, which also nurtured the aspirations of the times. Alur Venkatarayaru, Betageri Krishna Sharma, Bendre, Pa. Vem. Acharya and others charged the atmosphere of Hubli and Dharwad with their profound thoughts. In 1942, with the announcement of the *Chale Jaao* (Quit India) movement, the freedom struggle gained new momentum in Dharwad. The streets would be filled with students shouting slogans and brandishing flags. Protests and hunger strikes became the order of the day.

Even as Gangubai was not disconnected from any of this, she did not go down to the streets and join the movement. On her music expeditions, whenever she got an opportunity to visit Delhi, she made sure she stayed with her friend close to the Birla House where Gandhiji used to hold his prayer meetings. "Every evening I went for the prayer meeting and bhajans. It gave me a moral equilibrium." Gangubai, who refused to sing any lighter forms of music, sang a patriotic song composed by her dear friend N.K. from AIR Bombay on 15 August 1947: *Bharatiya Svatantrada Sooryanindu Belagiha.*

When the entire nation was reeling under the shock of Gandhiji's death, Gangubai's experience was no different—she was bereft. Much later, her son Babanna mentioned that, after Gandhiji's death, she went to Triveni Sangam, Allahabad, where his ashes had been immersed. Despite much prodding, Gangubai wouldn't talk about this. She was like that about several things—her feelings were very private. For her, the death of Gandhi was not only a national loss, it was also personal. He was the force that gave her the staying power to carry on against all odds with equanimity.

She associated India's freedom with the death of her guru soon after: "He died too soon after India attained independence. Had he lived longer he would have won so many awards. If I, being his disciple, got so many honours, imagine what he would have been showered with!"

During the heyday of the Indian freedom struggle, the social climate of Hubli–Dharwad opened up new worlds for Gangubai. Her association with contemporary progressive writers and thinkers, and friendship with activists like Patil Puttappa kept alive her social consciousness. This, along with her own reading habit, and the life she was living shaped Gangubai into an unusual personality. For a musician of her calibre, she was utterly simple and had place for everyone in her home, even passers-by. She articulated herself best through her music. The figure of Gangubai became a creative outlet for ascendant nationalistic feelings, then, while her music in turn expressed everything her personality embodied—music was Gangubai's language.

Whenever she set out on a concert tour, she would make sure she had enough books to last her entire journey. When she went to Bombay, she would always rent the same small room on the first floor of a printing press. Plenty of Marathi books came to the press for binding. "I could read and speak fluent Marathi. The people who worked in the press had become my friends, and no sooner would I land there than they would say, 'Here are the new books. Read them in a day and return them.' I would sit reading late into the night, and go back for more the next morning," she would remember fondly. In those days, Gangubai had even sheltered many a freedom fighter in her tiny little kholi, which she and Ramanna occupied. Much later, when a circulating library came up in Deshpande Nagar, she became one of its first members. She loved novels and had read almost every writer in Kannada. In fact, she loved thrillers and investigative novels, and would book them in advance. She would always admonish Krishna, whom she lovingly called Kitty, for not reading enough. "I could not read English. But I managed to read a few words, in conference booklets. For instance, my name, the name of the raga, names of some other musicians … That's about it." She was also a regular reader of *Prapancha*, a journal launched in Hubli in 1954 and edited by Patil Puttappa. Covering politics and society, the journal responded to many current issues.

For Gangubai, her ideas of right and wrong, and good and evil were intricately linked to what was good for her fellow human beings. Whenever Hubli was in trouble, and Gangubai felt something was unjust or unfair, she came out to protest. For instance, in 1953, when

B.V. Keskar became the minister of Information and Broadcasting, a committee formed under the chairmanship of S.N. Ratanjankar decided to reaudition all the artistes who had been performing for All India Radio all those years. Except Mallikarjun Mansur and Gangubai Hangal, everyone else was going to be regraded. Both these musicians took the lead in fighting this humiliating move, and organized a picketing campaign. This had widespread repercussions and resulted in agitation across the stations of the country. They sat in protest along with the artiste fraternity in front of the Dharwad station. The committee, just to prove its might, forcibly conducted auditions for a few artistes. After a few months of standoff, AIR, on its own, increased the fee for artistes and started issuing contracts to all artistes like before.

Gangubai became the voice of peace and harmony when the Idgah Maidan episode resurfaced in the 1990s. The dispute over the ownership of Idgah Maidan in Hubli dates back to the 1970s. When the RSS and its leaders descended on Hubli to "reclaim" it as their territory, a Hindu–Muslim riot erupted there. Firing ensued and people were killed. Twenty years later, when she narrated this episode to me, the horror of the incident continued to assail her—she was witness to the murder of her neighbour's son, an innocent teenager. "Did Hindu and Muslim gods war with each other? Why are they not our own?" she asked me. "In music, we have learnt that they are all one. We sing in praise of Allah just as we sing the glory of Saraswati. Bismillah is my brother, and he is an ardent worshipper of Kashi Vishwanatha. Why are we doing this to each other?" Gangubai, who was then a member of the Rajya Sabha, raised this issue in the House, asking "Are there greater and lesser gods?" To me she said, "I could not control myself … I broke down."

Gangubai never understood the politics of hate or exclusion. She wasn't even a politically correct speaker. She had a typical "village" mindset, according to which everyone was everyone's business. She would throw herself into a situation and take moral responsibility for it. As was wont, political forces did not lose the opportunity to brand her as the secular face of the country. The picture in which she lovingly embraces Bismillah Khan became the poster representative of communal harmony in the SAARC Summit held in Bangalore after the Babri Masjid demolition.

* * *

Gururaj Kaulgi, Gangubai's husband, was an affectionate man. He lived with his parents and his wife, but spent considerable time even in Gangubai's household. Since he was a connoisseur of music, he was never an impediment in her musical career. He also knew that music was her sole support, the bread of her life and soul. From the beginning, it was Ramanna who stood firmly with Gangubai, accompanying her to every concert. Himself a *tabaliya*, Ramanna had a keen musical sense and was her greatest critic. There are wonderful stories about how he would sit in the very first row at every concert of Gangubai's, and she would constantly look towards him for feedback, especially in the early minutes of the concert. Ramanna would send messages to her with the rise and fall of his hand, and she would immediately interpret the gesture. For the first few minutes, till the concert acquired its flow, Ramanna was Gangubai's beacon.

It was no mean task for Gangubai to bring up her three children. She was not in a position to give up her musical career and look after them. In the initial years, each time there was a concert or recording, she would leave the kids at her maternal uncle Krishnappa's house in Dharwad. She had to set out with enough time to catch the train to Dharwad, drop the kids at her uncle's house and progress with the journey. It was not easy. The only mode of transport for the journeys she undertook was train. This happened frequently, and the kids got so used to being in their *maami*'s (aunt's) care that they began to call their aunt *avva* (mother) and Gangubai *akka* (sister). Sometimes Gangubai took Krishna or Babu along with her. The kids would be in somebody's care backstage when she would begin her concert. "How often I heard them crying … My heart would be with them, but I couldn't allow my music to fail either," she would say.

Years went by and the number of programmes Gangubai did increased, which also meant travelling more frequently than before. She could no longer sustain the arrangement of travelling to Dharwad to drop off the kids. By this time, it so happened that Krishnappa *maama* lost his job. She requested him to shift to Hubli with his wife and kids. She would take care of them while they in turn managed her children and home. Gangubai did try very hard to get Krishnappa *maama* a job, but it failed to materialize. So she ended up taking on their responsibility completely. Very soon Ramanna also got married and, since Gangubai was so totally dependent on him, his family also began to live with her. All the three families lived together. Gangubai had the huge responsibility of looking after a family of twenty members.

Making ends meet was a constant struggle. The kids had to be sent to school, they had to be fed, they required new clothes—it was endless. And, because of Gangubai's busy schedule, all the children, as a rule, joined school late and completed their education late. Whatever her difficulties were, she put them on the backburner and reminded the children again and again that there was no excuse for them to do badly in their studies.

Krishna was a weak child, and she suffered from frequent bouts of stomach ache. Gangubai's sons, Babu and Narayan, did well in school and in college. Babu did his master's in commerce and Nani became an engineer. Krishnappa *maama* and Ramanna's kids were not left behind either.

Gururaj Kaulgi was a law graduate from the University of Bombay. But, sadly, he never practised law. He seemed to get into various businesses, and suffered huge losses since he had no business acumen. He never offered Gangubai any monetary support, she always had to fend for herself. In addition, she had to carry the burden of clearing the financial mess he would get into. Whenever the topic of her marriage and her husband was raised, Gangubai would say with a calm face, "He was a good man, but he was not good at business. He could not help me much ...." Never could one find a trace of bitterness in her.

Kaulgi, who had some money on him, bought a house in Deshpande Nagar in 1943 for Rs 12,000, and asked Gangubai to move in with her family. The house was very small, and the rest of the plot was vacant. But they could not complain—at least they now had a house of their own. For nearly six years they had neither water nor electricity. They would fetch water from a nearby well or the handpump at the end of the street. It was a difficult period, but Gangubai loved the sense of togetherness and self-assurance she got from her extended family.

Gangubai was emotionally very vulnerable, and was given to brooding. She would worry endlessly over a small problem. In her autobiography she says, "Even a simple cold or cough would leave me anxious. Will this turn into typhoid or pneumonia? My fears would run riot and tire me out." But somehow, in the company of her loving aunts and uncles, all her apprehensions receded.

Once, in the early 1950s, a family friend who owned a petrol bunk decided to sell it. Gangubai heard of this and thought it would be good for her husband to take over the business. She sold the very small piece of land she had in Hubli and bought the petrol bunk for her husband. He started off well, Gangubai was happy that she could do something to boost his self-confidence. Within no time he incurred huge losses and they were forced to sell the bunk. With this, Gangubai not only lost whatever little she had, but was also saddled with huge amounts of debt.

Upon completing his education, her son Babanna took on the role of her manager and even accompanied her to concerts. For twenty-two years they had all lived together. By then, Gangubai had helped Ramanna set up a flour mill and a firewood depot. Inevitably, as his children grew up, the demands of his family had increased. Gangubai had been finding it very difficult to cope. Her grandmother, who was still alive and lived with Gangubai those years, often advised her not to take on so much responsibility. "Maama must be on his own now. Let him look after his family," she would say. But this was never easy for Gangubai. "If the word 'burden' means money, then one should not let it cause one so much unhappiness. I could live with the bare minimum, so I told myself that this would continue as long as it was possible for me," she explained. Ramanna meant a lot to her. "I had no great ambitions. I never aspired for a bungalow, a huge car, or jewellery … But why should everybody else be like me? I knew there was not enough money coming in, and I could not afford them a life of great comfort. I didn't want to make them unhappy. If I had postponed this any longer, it may not have been good for any of us." In 1954, Ramanna and his family moved into a house of their own.

The house that Kaulgi bought had plenty of vacant land. Gangubai told Ramanna to build a house there. "We separated on very good terms. There was no unpleasantness," she said. They were now on their own, but as far as Gangubai was concerned nothing had changed. For every little thing Gangubai had to run to Ramanna. He was her confidant, and the one person with whom she could share her joys and sorrows. It wasn't any different for Ramanna. She was his dear niece and he treasured her. Their bond of love and affection remained until Ramanna's end.

* * *

Gangubai was a woman of magnanimous temperament and extraordinary goodness. Unusually, Gururaj Kaulgi's parents—orthodox Brahmins who weren't too happy about their son marrying a lower-caste girl—became extremely fond of Gangubai. They would get restless if they didn't see her every now and then. "Why hasn't she come to visit us?" they would enquire. She had very cordial relations with Kaulgi's wife as well. Since Gangubai was older to her, the lady called her *akka*. Gangubai was very fond of their kids, and they too, in turn, looked up to their *chikkamma* (little mother) with enormous affection. Whenever she bought anything for the kids at home, she included Kaulgi's other kids as well. She never lost sight of them.

In fact, Gangubai had a very cordial relationship with her father's first wife as well. She called her *dodda aai* (elder mother).

The lady was a devotee of the god Mylaralinga, and whenever she visited the hilltop temple, she took Gangu along. She knew that Gangu did not like the *prasada* or the food given at the temple, and therefore she always woke up early to make rice for Gangu and packed it for her to eat later. *Dodda aai* was asthmatic and suffered severe attacks. It was her sister at Kenkoti who always nursed her back to health. "My father's sons were all well educated. One was an engineer, the other a banker, and the third worked for the army. My father didn't survive for too long after my mother's death. He died a year after … I used to meet his children occasionally …" her memories were vivid.

"My father knew my husband was into business. He came to Hubli before he passed away. He took me aside and spoke to me for a long time. 'Are you happy, my dear?' he had asked me. 'If you have any difficulty leading your life, you should never hesitate to tell me, Gangu. I am your father, don't forget that. Don't even hesitate to come and stay in our Dharwad house,' he had said putting his hand around my shoulder. He was a nice person, very fond of music …" she said trailing off.

Gangubai would often recall with sadness how her mother's death changed many things. She had to let go of the little indulgences that were her prerogative. "I could only throw a tantrum with my mother I would quarrel with her for every little thing. Despite all her difficulties, she would pamper me for I was her only child. When she died, I suddenly felt like an elderly, responsible woman at eighteen. I began to go around with a big boulder on my head."

* * *

With Ramanna taking on new responsibilities and shaping his own life, Gangubai was left with no one else to escort her and handle her programmes. By the time her children grew up, she was a famous, sought-after musician. There were more invitations from various parts of the country, and more recordings were scheduled. Babanna, who had initially accompanied her on concert tours, couldn't continue with the responsibility. Someone had to be there at home. He began to manage all her affairs—her correspondence and finances. He would brief her about concert invitations, recordings and travel, and carry out her instructions. "My mother was not worldly-wise. Despite all our difficulties she was not particular about money. There were some artistes who were extremely rigid about their fee. For instance, Kesarbai Kerkar and Faiyaz Khan would refuse to sing if the organizers even made an attempt to bargain. They would specify an amount that had to be paid. But my mother was just the opposite. If they said, 'Bai ... can you reduce a bit. We are in a bit of a tight spot,' just the next instant she would say, 'Okay, okay, pay whatever you can,' and would put an end to the matter," recalled Babanna.

The remuneration she received would never be on par with that of the male artistes who had a similar stature as she. Since she came from a small town, she was inept at negotiating these matters. Ramanna was equally bad—a naive village bumpkin who loved music and was awestruck by the strides his niece was making in the musical firmament. Many organizers took advantage of her nature. They would ask her which class she would like to travel by, when she would say, "Inter is good enough." Inter, in those days, was a class above third class. She did many programmes for SPICMACAY, which only took care of her board and lodging. She went to remote places all over Maharashtra and Gujarat, and sang in various schools and colleges. "Not even once would she complain to them about her accommodation or the lack of any facility. She was very busy and could easily have refused to do these lec-dem programmes. She was the most non-fussy musician, extremely serious about her art," Babanna explained. "I used to be greatly moved by my mother's simplicity."

Once, Gangubai went to AIR Delhi for a recording. It was scheduled for 8.30 a.m. and, being as disciplined as she was, she turned up well before time. "My mother, with her ordinary looks and her nine-yard sari, perhaps looked like a curious villager who had wandered into the station. The guard stopped my mother and asked her to sit on the parapet wall near the gate, even though she told him

With her daughter Krishna in the 1930s

Pt. Sawai Gandharva

Gururaj Kaulgi

A young Gangu

Pt. Sawai Gandharva (centre) with his disciples Krishnabai Ramdurgkar and Gangubai Hangal seated next to him. On the extreme right is Krishna Hangal and on the far left is Pt. Bhimsen Joshi.

Seated: (from second left)
Pt. Bhimsen Joshi, Gangubai Hangal and the sculptor Chawate

Standing: (from left) Chawate's brother, Pt. Shripad Padigar and Pt. Madhav Gudi

With Pt. Bhimsen Joshi

With Krishna

With Prime Minister Indira Gandhi

With Da. Ra. Bendre (1896–1981) and family friend R.V. Bijur

Gangubai and Krishna with Pt. Ravi Shankar

(clockwise from left) With Pt. Jasraj, with Ustad Bismillah Khan, and with the Kannada superstar Dr Rajkumar

Top: Receiving the Padma Bhushan at Rashtrapati Bhavan

Left: Gangubai's childhood home in Dharwad, now a museum

Bottom: On her 93rd birthday, in her Hubli home, Ganga Lahari

Honorary doctorate degree at the eighth Annual Convocation of Karnataka State Open University (KSOU), 2008

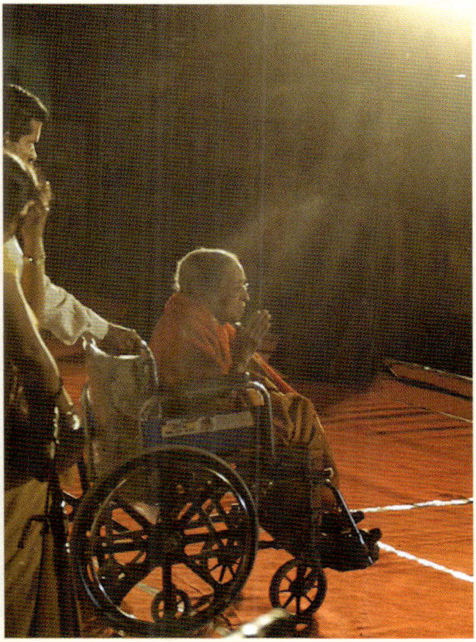

Receiving guests from her wheelchair at the annual Sawai Gandharva All Night Music Festival in Kundagol

Tuning her tanpura at her home, Ganga Lahari

Walking towards the main hall of her home in Hubli

that she had come there for a recording," narrated Babanna. Soon, the station director arrived and was surprised to see her sitting at the gate. "Baiji, why are you waiting here?" he looked embarrassed. "This is where your guard asked me to sit, I did what I was told to," she quipped. "God, save us, save us …" he mumbled, beating his forehead with his palm. Casting an angry look at the guard, he quickly took her inside. "How does it matter to him who I am? Nor did I feel like telling him. It's not his mistake, he was doing his work," she had consoled the station director.

Babanna tried his hand at music for some years. He sang light music at AIR for nearly five years, but gave it up soon. "I found it very difficult to carry on. My mother was such an outstanding musician that my amateurish singing, I thought, would bring discredit to her," he explained.

Having stepped into Ramanna's role, it was difficult for Babanna to step out of it. His brother Narayan had found a job with PWD and moved to Haveri. Babanna had dreams of having his own job, an independent life, but Gangubai feigned ignorance. She did not encourage him to look for a job, though she never spelt it out in any clear terms. So Babanna became his mother's secretary. Initially, he had to accompany her on concert tours, but once Krishna started accompanying her mother he didn't have to.

Kaulgi remained completely out of all this. Every problem that cropped up in her family life had to be resolved by Gangubai herself. He was an affectionate man, but was rather indifferent to the needs of the household. "He was helpful by nature. But he had seen that the people who came to him during their difficulties turned their back on him once their job was done. Once, Ramanna's son had failed in his exams and was so depressed that he stopped attending college. We hadn't yet discussed this with my husband, because he came to our house once in a while—and why burden him with our problems? But he got to know. He took the poor child out, spoke to him gently, and convinced him to go back to his studies," she remembered. Another time, Ramanna's youngest son wandered off to play with his friends after school, and Kaulgi went looking for him, bringing him back by car. Since he had a motor business, there were always many cars at his disposal. "He was very fond of my *maama*'s kids, Uma and Raju. He took them with him all the time. If people asked him, 'Are these your kids?' he would say, 'yes'—that's how he was. Unfortunately, he did not do well in his own business," she would say dolefully. She had no expectations from Kaulgi. Her love for him was unconditional. She carried on with her duties with a missionary zeal. Music was her shield.

Lest Gangubai forget that she was riding a roller coaster, one small happy moment would be followed by a hundred problems. Out of the blue, one afternoon, Gangubai received a notice from the bank stating the seizure of her house. It was as if a thunderbolt had hit her! Kaulgi, who had raised a loan to purchase this little house, had become a defaulter with the bank; he hadn't repaid them. Gangubai didn't have a single penny on her. Making ends meet was an ordeal—how was she ever going to save anything! How was she going to save the house? Where would she go with the entire family—children, aunts and uncles?

The house came up for auction. Gangubai knew that she was on the streets and had lost all hope of any luck coming her way. On the day of the auction, someone knocked at her door fairly early in the morning. It was Upendra Naik, a well-wisher and connossieur of her music from Udupi. She had no interest in meeting anyone, but welcomed him out of courtesy and offered him tea. Five minutes later, the gentleman announced the purpose of his visit: he had heard about the auction and was there to buy the house for her. "Leave your worries, Baiji, leave everything to me." He made a bid for the house, bagged the deal, and handed over the papers to Gangubai. Gangubai broke down and wept like never before. "When do I repay you?" she asked the good Samaritan. "Whenever you can," he had said. "I was not stranded, after all," she would say, wiping her tears. "He was truly a godsend. In my moments of crisis, some unanticipated help has always come my way … I repaid him in due course of time."

"Even when she was let down so badly by my father, my mother would not speak a word. Whenever we recalled that episode, she would express her gratitude for Upendra Naik. She was a woman of tremendous inner strength. Her attitude towards my father remained unchanged in spite of all the difficulties he put her through," Babanna mused, continuing to be perplexed at her ability to absorb hardships.

In 1962, Babanna got married to Lalitha, who was the daughter of a landlord in Chikkodi. A common friend of the two families had made this proposal to Gangubai's uncle, but he had refused saying the girl was too fat. But when Gangubai came to know of this, she insisted that they consider the proposal seriously. "What if she is fat? What does one do with good looks? I want a nice girl for my son," she argued with her uncle. Once things began to move, Lalitha's father began to have his own apprehensions. He belonged to a generation that did not think too highly of a musician's family, moreover it was a huge household. He didn't want to make his daughter's life difficult. But the marriage was destined to take place. The household, its many expectations, a mother-in-law constantly on tour—Lalitha realized that circumstances weren't rosy. But both Gangubai and Kaulgi won her over with affection. Kaulgi wanted his daughter-in-law to learn English, so he appointed a Christian teacher and sent Lalitha by car to learn from him.

Babanna and Lalitha, like every other young couple, had their own aspirations. Once again, Babanna gently tried asking his mother if he could apply for a job. Gangubai was worried, and did not give him the go-ahead. If Babanna went away, she wouldn't have a family and neither would she have someone to take care of the household. She remained indifferent to his pleas. The younger son was away. If Babanna were to also go away, how would she cope? Gangubai was very fortunate that she had children who loved their mother dearly. They had great respect for her. Even when they were at a disadvantage, they never made a noise about it. "It never came to an exchange of words. The children understood their mother and never crossed the line that she drew for them," Lalitha would say.

* * *

Kaulgi fell ill. He would seem to recover, and then fall ill again. His health was failing steadily. In 1966, Kaulgi took ill rather seriously. Gangubai had a scheduled concert in Bombay, but she wanted to stay back. She had almost decided to cancel the concert, but Kaulgi insisted that she go. Gangubai and Krishna left with a heavy heart. They left Hubli, and Kaulgi's health worsened. The following day, which was the day of her concert, Kaulgi passed away. "We sent her a telegram, she wasn't informed about it during the concert, however. I had to finish the rites the very same day. My friends came to my help, and my brother who was working in Haveri rushed to Hubli. By the time my mother returned, it was all over," Babanna remembered sadly.

Play of light and shade

Babanna and Lalithakka anchored Gangubai's life. Krishna was more than a daughter to her. She not only became her musical companion, but was also a friend. Even though they were dependent on each other in many ways, neither of them opened their hearts to each other. They were close, understood each other's requirements, and deeply cared for each other. At times they got angry with each other, sulked and stopped talking, but would patch up very soon as well. Despite the closeness, Krishna never overstepped boundaries—she was intimidated by her mother. This was true of most of Gangubai's intimate relationships, but Krishna's and hers needs a special mention, because they shared that extra-special bond—of music, and of friendship.

Babanna had four children, of them two sons and two daughters—Manoj, Arun, Madhavi and Anita (Vaishnavi). Narayan also had two sons—Mahesh and Dinesh—and a daughter, Lakshmi. By now, Krishnappa *maama*'s son, Seshagiri Hangal, had been groomed into a competent tabla player and began to accompany his aunt. Gangubai had a soft corner for Seshagiri, who had lost a leg to polio. The handicap never became a deterrent for Seshu, who lived his life as actively as other "normal" human beings. Gangubai, given her nature, showered him with extra love and attention. Alongside Gangubai were Krishna and Seshu, while on the harmonium Vasant Kanakapur and sometimes Appa Jalgaonkar accompanied her. People close to her often asked, "Why do you always take Seshu with you? Won't people think you are promoting your own family members?" In reply Gangubai would say, "Let them say whatever pleases them. If I don't give him that push, nobody else will. Moreover, he is very talented." Eventually, Seshu went on to become a highly respected tabla player.

Things hadn't changed much after Ramanna's family moved out. The house was still full. Babanna's children, Seshu's children, and Krishna even brought her uncle's son to live with them. While Gangubai was constantly on tour, Babanna took care of all the mundane demands of the household—paying bills, managing correspondence, repairs and finances—while Lalitha took charge of the kitchen and the children.

Whenever Gangubai and Krishna were at home, they would help with the household chores. Krishna would buy the daily supply of vegetables, and tend to the kitchen. Gangubai was very particular about cleaning the rice. She would not trust anyone else doing it. Even at ninety, when she had poor eyesight and no strength in her scrawny fingers, she would wear her glasses, sit by the window and clean the rice: a ritual that lasted a couple of hours. "When she went out of town, she would clean a minimum of five kilos, fill it into a separate box and keep it ready for use," recalls Lalitha, beaming. Gangubai also had a way with vegetables: she would clean and cut them like they have been run through a precision instrument, all ready for the day's cooking.

Much of the cooking in Gangubai's house had been Brahminized. It was probably because of her father and her husband. In fact, Ambabai stopped cooking meat after coming into contact with Nadiger. The food prepared in Gangubai's kitchen was a typical North Karnataka, vegetarian meal. Alla Rakha, Ravi Shankar, Hirabai—whoever visited Gangubai's house loved the food. "Ravi Shankar has written in his book that I make the best *rasam.* Have you read it? The day he came, it wasn't I who had made the *rasam* ..." she would break into laughter, covering her mouth with the edge of her sari. Once, Hirabai refused to leave without the recipe. She walked straight into the kitchen, sat on the kitchen stool and said, *Ab bolo, kaise karna hai?* "She didn't know Kannada, and I didn't know enough Hindi to give her a recipe. I knew conversational Hindi, but didn't know the names of cooking ingredients. Finally, I had to put all the ingredients in a plate and hold it before her, and tell her the measure of each." Apparently Hirabai teased her about her mannerisms when she sang, saying that her gestures were extremely domestic and brought to mind activities like roasting, frying, rolling, etc.! "Was there any escape from domesticity for me?" she would say jovially. "Maybe I did worry a lot about food, and it infiltrated into my musical mannerisms as well."

Gangubai loved her grandchildren and fussed over them endlessly. Whenever she sat down to make butter, she would dip her fingers into the yellow, creamy fresh butter that floated up in a vessel, and called out to all her grandchildren, offering one finger to each of them. Kittakka, as the kids called Krishna, was an equally indulgent aunt. She played with them, fed them, bathed them, and behaved like she was one of them. There was a constant supply of *avalakki chuda* (beaten rice garnished with dry coconut, curry leaves and peanuts) and *undi* (a sweet ball made from roasted wheat flour or besan, jaggery and *ghee*) for the children. Once the mixture for *undi* was roasted, Gangubai would press them into balls and fill them into a big box. Whenever they left Hubli for a concert, she would ensure that there was enough for the children and guests till she returned. She always carried some with her as well.

Come what may, every festival had to be celebrated. Gangubai and Krishna would walk to the market and buy all the supplies. Gangubai never took a bus or an auto, but walked, because that way she could save some money. The household being large, they needed a substantial quantity of groceries and vegetables, they would return loaded with bags. Once in a while, if any of her grandchildren insisted on going along with her, she would bring them back by bus. There would be new clothes for the children, and a special meal would be cooked. She would help in making all the special dishes.

Gangubai worked very hard for her family and took care of its members with great affection. Whatever her difficulty, she would never make it known to them. When Babanna's wife Lalitha was expecting, Gangubai did not permit her to go to her maternal home. Each time, Lalitha's parents came to seek the grand old lady's permission, but she promptly turned them down. Gangubai feared that there wouldn't be proper facilities in the village and made sure that she herself took care of her. "She bathed the newborn and me, cooked a separate meal for me, and also took care of the other children. Till I was fit to get back to my normal routine, she would do everything. She would walk to the hospital two to three times each day, carrying my food. They were difficult times and with so many mouths to feed, it was tough. For all that she has done for me and my children, whatever I do in return will not measure up," Lalithakka's eyes would turn moist.

Whenever Gangubai and Krishna went to Delhi, they stayed with Susheela Ambike, a close friend of Gangubai's. Susheela, a professor of Sanskrit, had a deep and abiding interest in music. She was also a sensitive friend and understood Gangubai's predicament completely. Susheela accompanied them everywhere—to concerts, to the market, to meet people … In fact, for most of Gangubai's SPICMACAY concerts, Susheela took over the lecture part and Gangubai did the demonstration. When Gangubai went to Delhi to receive the Padma Bhushan and Padma Vibhushan, Susheela went with her. "Gangubai never went back without buying clothes for the children. In the 1950s, I had friends in the Delhi Cloth Mills. You could buy cloth at a cheaper price there. Gangubai would buy for her kids, Ramanna's kids, Kaulgi's kids, and Krishna's *maama*'s kids, reams and reams of the same kind of cloth. Later, she started buying for her grandchildren as well. Everyone got the same stuff," remembers Susheela, who was close to Gangubai till her very end. The kids were teased by being called the "Hangal Pant Company"—boys and girls always shared the same material and print.

It was lovely for the kids to have such an indulgent grandmother. At the same time, she was also clear about drawing the necessary lines. She determined most things for them, given that she was the matriarch of the family. She would never beat the kids or scold them. She rarely raised her voice but, if she did, it was enough of a reprimand to get the kids crying. They were so fond of her, that even the slightest displeasure they caused her would make them penitent. Since Gangubai took on every responsibility, the others took it rather easy. This was true even of simple things. For instance, Lalitha would ask, "What should I cook today?"

She sent all her grandchildren to good schools, and ensured that there were no hindrances in their studies. Kittakka would save money to buy the children new sets of uniforms and books. When the examinations approached, both mother and daughter would worry endlessly. On the day of the results, Gangubai and Krishna would be the first to wake up. After a quick bath, they would rush to the school to see the results. The children always did well, bringing Gangubai and Krishna much joy. They would walk to the market, buy one or two boxes of the famous Dharwad *pedha* and go home. They would then take the children to school in a car, so that they too could see their results. "There used to be such a festive air, it was unbelievable. It was just short of a coronation, as if we had topped our IAS exams," reminisces Gangubai's granddaughter Vaishnavi.

With her busy schedule, Gangubai kept a constant vigil. Everyone had to be back home by 6.30 p.m. The girls would never be sent on school trips and, of course, they couldn't talk to boys. Even if Lalitha spoke to a stranger, Gangubai would get jittery. "Who was that? Why were you talking to him? What did he say?"—a hundred questions would follow. She was not in the least narrow-minded or conservative, but was simply overprotective.

Gangubai disliked being alone. It would grip her with a strange fear. Once, on a train journey, there wasn't anyone else in the compartment. She climbed up the berths and anxiously pulled out the bulb. Whenever she was alone, she preferred to sit in darkness. She did this even at home. This is why everyone rushed back home before 7 p.m.

* * *

Unexpectedly, in early 1971, a couple of government officers came to Gangubai's house. Gangubai was away for a concert and was supposed to return the following day. They met Ramanna, who lived next door, and told him that Gangubai had been awarded the Padma Bhushan. They had come there to collect her consent letter. Ramanna, overjoyed by this news, took the consent letter and offered to get it signed. He was eagerly waiting for his dear niece's return. No sooner did she arrive than Ramanna ran over to her house and got the consent letter signed. In those days, the Padma awards were announced on 26 January, but All India Radio usually announced it on 25 January in their late-night bulletin. Gangubai and Ramanna sat glued to their radio set. Nothing was announced in the 9 p.m. news capsule. They quickly finished their dinner, and came back to listen to the last news of the day at 11 p.m. Even then there was no report about the award. Both Gangubai and Ramanna were disappointed, but without saying much they returned to their respective homes. A little past midnight, a cycle bell rang at her door piercing the stillness of the night. A voice called out, "Telegram, telegram." All kinds of bad thoughts came to her and she rushed to the door. She shouted out to Ramanna and, not having slept yet, he ran out immediately. She handed over the telegram to him and he read it out loud. "Congratulations on your Padma Bhushan award—Indira Gandhi."

Gangubai broke down. The first person she remembered was her mother. She then remembered her guru, Sawai Gandharva. Both these people who probably would have been overjoyed by this were not with her. That entire night, Ramanna and Gangubai sat recalling their past—their joys, sorrows, ups and downs. Mataldinni, a family friend and well-wisher, had returned to Hubli on the morning of 26 January at 4 a.m. He had bought a newspaper at the railway station and was delighted to learn that Gangubai had been conferred the Padma Bhushan. With a copy of the newspaper, he went straight to their house and congratulated her. "I cannot forget the expression on his face that day. It was as if he had won the award," Gangubai joked.

Life went on as usual. In the years after the Padma Bhushan, Ramanna fell ill. In 1974, he died at the age of sixty-seven. After this, Gangubai had no one to open her heart to. With Ramanna's death, curtains were drawn on a major chapter in her life. One by one, her inner circle had dwindled. All those who came to live with her from her mother's times were gone. Ramanna was the last of them.

In the following years, Gangubai made yet another valuable friendship. In the early 1970s, she visited Delhi for a concert. After her stunning recital that day, a lady came up to her and spoke in Kannada. She told her how happy her music had made her. The gentleman who had followed the lady also told her the same. Gangubai was thrilled to listen to Kannada in the Hindi heartland. The man was none other than H.Y. Sharada Prasad, advisor to the Prime Minister, and the lady was his graceful wife, Kamalamma. Gangubai knew of Sharada Prasad, but had never met the man. "Henceforth, whenever you come to Delhi, you should visit us. You can even stay with us if you so wish," they told her. And sure enough, Gangubai did spend a lot of time with them each time she visited Delhi. She was a very easy guest, took care of herself, and made no demands whatsoever. Gangubai integrated well with the family, and would chat with them about everyday things. Sometimes she would regale them with stories about other musicians. She would speak a lot about Kesarbai Kerkar—since they both came from similar backgrounds, but also formed two ends of the spectrum in terms of their personas, Gangubai was quite charmed by her. Kesarbai Kerkar was a good twenty years older, but everyone who met her was stunned into silence by her airs of an empress! Gangubai never spoke about her music or her own difficulties.

Every now and then she would call Sharada Prasad from Hubli, and seek his advice on many things. Sharada Prasad, too, thought very highly not only of Gangubai and her art, but also of her genuineness and simplicity as a person. He would say, "She looks like a little sparrow, but if she opens her mouth she transforms into a roaring lion!"

Sharada Prasad wanted Gangubai to meet Prime Minister Indira Gandhi. So he fixed a breakfast appointment with her at the Prime Minister's residence. Seshu and Krishna went along as well. Breakfast was served and, when they were about to have tea, Indira Gandhi joined them. First, Sharada Prasad offered an introduction, "I learn, a lot of interest in Hindustani music is being shown in Karnataka these days," Indira Gandhi remarked casually, at which Gangubai retorted, "Much of the country's Hindustani music has been the contribution of Karnataka." Recalling the meeting, Gangubai told me, "Whoever it maybe, when people make such flippant remarks, I get upset. Musicians don't get made overnight. It takes decades …"

Sharada Prasad was a man of letters, and often wrote to Gangubai. These would be about her recent radio concert, a recording, or something else he wished to share with her. He was such a meticulous man that he even made notes of his meetings with Gangubai. One such letter describes in detail Gangubai's recording for India's Cultural Festival in Germany.

In 1978, Gangubai was awarded an honorary doctorate from Karnatak University. Subsequently, she even got more doctorates from the universities of Gulbarga, Hampi and Delhi. She called Sharada Prasad: "Dr Gangubai Hangal here. If you have any ailments, please let me know, you shall be treated by this doctor," she had said in her characteristically simple householder's humour.

Even though Gangubai travelled often and widely, she was always in a hurry to get back. Fellow musicians always asked her, "Do you have many programmes in Hubli? Is that why you are always in such a hurry to rush back?" That was not the case. Gangubai performed more in Maharashtra and North India than she did in Hubli or the rest of Karnataka. But somehow, she always longed to be in Hubli. "I don't leave Hubli and Hubli doesn't leave me," she would say. A person of similar temperament was Ustad Bismillah Khan. He refused to leave Kashi. Once, when an organizer asked him to come for a performance outside the country, he had famously asked: "Does the Ganga flow there? Do you have a Vishwanath Temple in your place?"

"Every street in Hubli, every nook and corner, the marketplace, the people—I am so familiar with this place. It gives me a sense of security to be here," Gangubai would say. For her, it was always important to be in the company of the people she knew, to share the warmth of that community. That is probably why, whenever she went out of Hubli, she asked the organizers to put her up is someone's house rather than a hotel. "There's a sense of anonymity in a hotel, and I don't feel comfortable," she would reason. "When I walk on the streets of Hubli, someone or the other comes up to talk to me. When I walk home from the market, autodrivers stop for me, '*Bayare*, please get in, I'll drop you,' they offer. If I were living anywhere else, would this have happened?" As the train came closer to Hubli station, her heart would pound with excitement. She would look out of the window every few seconds as the train chugged into the station, peeping to see who had come to take her home. "Oh God! How I would long to get back home!" Getting philosophical, she would explain: "It is all preordained. It never occurred to me that I must leave Hubli for more money. It's also true that I never desired wealth."

The doors of Gangubai's house were never shut, literally and metaphorically. It is true even today. People keep walking in and out. During the evenings that Gangubai sat down for her *riyaz*, passers-by would peep in and ask, "*Bayare*, it's so long since we listened to you. Can we come in?" Of course, they were welcome. She would tell her grandchildren, "A musician's mind must be clean, free of calculations. If you are always thinking of profit and loss, then your music will not be good. That I use my art for a living is ironic." This was Gangubai's general outlook towards life: she never reduced anything to a table of loss and gain. In her relationships as well she never looked for any tangible benefits. Her relationship to Kaulgi was one example of this attitude. In her life emotion trumped pragmatism.

All her contemporaries, be they Bhimsen Joshi, Pt. Jasraj or Allah Rakha, knew how to get things done. They were capable of making demands, and also made sure the artiste was given his due. There are several stories of how musicians have walked out just before the concert, because the organizers had not made their payment in full. But Gangubai had no such worldly ceremoniousness. She did not know how to market herself, nor did she know how to demand her fee. She always remained underpaid.

One hears such stories only from those who were part of her immediate world. If you asked her whether she was paid well, she would say: "Oh yes, they gave me enough money." If you turned the question around and said, "But I suppose the male musicians were paid better?" she would say: "How should I know? I never asked them. Only once, when Kumar Gandharva and I went for a performance in Amritsar, the organizers pulled a fast one on us. But both of us suffered …" The narration of this incident was certainly not an answer to the question, but that was how she handled several questions. To me it seemed off the tangent but, I suppose, all she wanted to say was, "So what if they got paid more?"

The incident happened during an open-air programme in Amritsar under a *pandal.* To the organizers' dismay, it rained heavily. The programme was postponed to the next day in a nearby hall. They performed to a packed audience but, by the end of the concert, they came to realize that the organizers had vanished without paying them. Gangubai and Kumar Gandharva were left in the lurch, and neither of them had any money on them. Finally, they took a tonga to AIR, where they had a recording, completed it, collected their remuneration, bought their train tickets and reached home. "A month later, the organizers sent us a cheque of Rs 150 each. They were not bad people, but the rain caused them much trouble. Nobody cheated me," she would say, putting an end to that conversation.

Close friends like Susheela Ambike would often be intrigued by her silence on her husband and her father. She was so simple a person that these matters could not be settled by right and wrong.

She accepted her reality without resignation. Perhaps there was something more to her silence: her children signed as B.G. Hangal, N.G. Hangal and K.G. Hangal, where the G stood for Gangubai. She never attached her husband's name to hers.

* * *

The New York Academy invited Gangubai for a series of twenty-three concerts in the United States in 1979. When Gangubai left with Seshu, Krishna and Appa Jalgaonkar, hundreds had gathered at the Hubli station to see them off. The poet Bendre was there too. About the visit, she said: "Unlike our audience they would never clap in the middle of a performance. One is so used to an appreciative nod, a *wah*, *shabash* and all that, that when you sing for them you really don't know if you have been able to establish a rapport at all. You have to wait till the end of the performance to know their response. If they had really enjoyed the recital, they would give me a standing ovation lasting a couple of minutes." This, in fact, was among the key reasons that triggered her homesickness. "I am so used to our audience's response."

There, she gave an interview to Voice of America. The interview could not take place in English, hence it was done in Hindi. But Gangubai generously mixed Marathi and even a smattering of Kannada. The interview was mostly about her early years and how she came to learn music. As usual, she narrated her story through the two constants in her life—her mother, Ambabai, and her guru, Sawai Gandharva. "It was a three-month-long trip, and by the end I was just dying to get back. I was hungering for home food and I just could not go on. Nothing can give you the comfort of home—putting one's leg up and having a leisurely cup of chai ..."

Aparigraha

> The less you possess, the less you want, the better you are. And better for what? Not for your enjoyment of this life but for enjoyment of personal service to your fellow beings—service to which you dedicate yourself, body, soul and mind.
>
> —Mahatma Gandhi

The kitchen was at the centre of Gangubai's household: those who came into the house walked straight into it. It was here, at the dining table, that most conversations took place. A part of the kitchen was visible from Gangubai's room as well. In fact, the kitchen extended into Babanna and Lalithakka's room too. To make it more visually explicit, the kitchen is flanked by Babanna and Lalithakka's room on the one side and Gangubai's on the other. Even after Gangubai's passing away, the kitchen continues to be the emotional core of the house. Most of my conversations with Babanna and Lalithakka have taken place either at the dining table, or in front of the stove as Lalithakka set the water to boil for *jhunka*—a north Karnataka dish made from gram flour. Sometimes she would be roasting masala for sambar. I have listened to many of Manoj's inspired "speeches" while we had breakfast, during which he ran back and forth from the refrigerator urging me to taste a "divine mango *chutney*" or chilled watermelon. I cannot forget how, even when Gangubai was bedridden, her ears were firmly fixed to the kitchen—a place fuelled by her passion and energy. "Lalitha must be making *avalakki* for the kids," she would say from the sounds and smells that emanated from the kitchen.

And she would be right. Indeed, Lalithakka would be roasting peanuts for the evening's *avalakki*—beaten rice garnished with coconut and peanuts.

Lalithakka was in constant fear of Manoj's capricious largesse and Babanna's unbelievable goodness. What if there was nothing left for the next guest who would turn up? So, she would stack all the goodies—*chuda, laddoo*s, biscuits and other snacks—in her room, keeping them under her control. How often Lalithakka has told me, "Go, get a plate from the kitchen, also get a steel tumbler." She would drop some goodies into the plate and fill the glass with water from the steel jug that was on her table amidst tens of medicine bottles for her various ailments.

If food is a social signifier loaded with interpersonal and cultural meanings, Gangubai's household exemplified the definition. Food, in India, has always been at the centre of ritualistic practice, social behaviour and theological speculation. In Gangubai's home, one could see that food was eaten not only to satisfy hunger but also to strengthen the sense of community.

At my very first visit to their house, I recall that the gates were open. The courtyard was green, full of trees and shrubs: the *chikku* tree was overloaded with fruits, the hibiscus was bursting with flaming red flowers, those left behind from the morning's picking for the puja. The *nandi battalu* plant, a local variety of white blossoms, had snowy-white flowers here and there, still waiting to be touched by nature's seasonal benevolence. Much of the greenery in the courtyard was owing to its own natural willingness and not because of careful tending. The humid summer air hanging heavily around their house was a mixture of the dull fragrance of these flowers and the smell of boiling milk wafting from inside the house.

At the door, there was a heap of slippers. After leaving mine in what seemed to be a safe corner, I looked around and stepped in with trepidation. The house was full of people—teachers and students from a neighbouring school—and there was hardly any room to move around. In what was a sea of heads, I desperately tried to catch someone's attention and, in less than two minutes, a man of generous girth was hurriedly speeding towards the door with boxes of *pedha* stacked in hand. I stepped back, sticking myself to the gravelly wall by the side of the main door, "Come in, come in," he ushered me inside in a voice that was unmistakably friendly. Manoj Hangal, Gangubai's grandson, was in the thick of his grandmother's ninety-second birthday celebrations with nearly two hundred visitors. The museum, which was an extension of their modest home, was overpacked to nearly three times its capacity. No one has ever been able to escape Manoj's exceptional warmth and hospitality. Huge tea cans with paper cups followed soon after, carried by people who seemed like local versions of the famous Mona Lisa, the smile never fading from their faces.

Gangubai was carried in her chair into the courtyard from the adjoining entrance. She couldn't have possibly battled the upbeat crowd, waiting to see her from up close. She wore a striking red shawl with gold sequins. It was carefully adjusted like a "V", and every now and then she stuck her jaw into her neck, looked down at her shawl, and ran her spindly fingers over them. The few strands of hair left on her tiny head had been oiled and neatly tied into a bun with a yellow, plastic rubber band. Sitting in the shade of the *chikku* shrub, Gangubai looked pleased: her eyes swept through the courtyard and beyond the gate, and gleamed in happiness on seeing such a big gathering.

The cameras clicked away and Gangubai's toothless, affable smile egged the shutterbugs to take more pictures. Everyone sang for her and wished her, while she, in her natural, instinctive style, thanked them all and did not forget to say how much she loved Hubli. The speech was over, now it was time for tea and *pedha.* The next minute she was shakily calling out for Manoj and Babanna, hoping that at least one of them would turn up. She insisted that a box of *pedha*s be kept beside her. Everyone who walked up to her to say "bye" got an extra *pedha.*

After the crowd had cleared and *ajji* was moved into the house, she sank into her chair. A lady came with a pillow for her back.

"Were the *pedha*s enough? Did everyone get tea?" The lady merely nodded and went inside.

This episode left a firm imprint on my mind: that their home had space for everyone. That they were so genuinely hospitable they could put even a stranger at ease stirred me. In the following years, as I continued my association with the family, I have been increasingly surprised at their ability to take people into their fold. There was little order in the household, but there was always enough food for everyone. Lalithakka would have given me a cup of tea only ten minutes earlier, and Manoj would bring more. If I refused, he would get angry. *Eeki kudiyangilla andra voyri olaga, bekadasht mandi adara kudiyakka* ... (If she doesn't want it, take it back, there are plenty of people here to have chai …)" and would loudly slurp his tea. Precisely two minutes later, looking up grumpily from his cup, he would ask, "What? Should I get you some tea?" By then, I would have lost the courage to say "no". So many times, when I only had half an hour to leave for the station, Manoj would furiously honk from near the gate, "*Hatta* ... *bega* …" urging me to get on to his scooter. He would speed away to a nearby women's co-operative where *khadak rotti* and the sweet *mandige* were sold. He would buy some of both, and thrust the plastic bag into my hands. Even if a whisper that seemed like reluctance came out of me, he would hurl a long sentence at me expressing his irritation: "*Adakka ree* ... I won't come to Bangalore."

At the stroke of five in the evening, Babanna would bring tea for everyone in the house in porcelain cups, without even the customary asking. Five in the evening is a good time to have tea, and hence everyone got a cup—these were the assumptions upon which Gangubai's home ran. And there was always a cup or two extra, just in case someone walked in while the rest sipped away. I have never seen the door of their house shut: Babanna, the first one to wake up, would open the door at six, only to shut it late at night. Whenever I have reached Hubli well before the crack of dawn, Manoj has sleepily zipped me home on his scooter, and Babanna would be standing in front of the stove, boiling milk for tea. "Have a wash and come. Tea will be ready," his voice would pierce the morning silence.

Food never escaped any conversation with Gangubai. Not that she spoke of exotic, high cuisine, raving about and craving taste and temptation. The simplicity of her comestible desires was just as startling as that of her personality. If the conversation was about her early days, she would inevitably bring to mind Ustad Abdul Karim Khan saying, *Beti, khoob khana aur khoob gana.* Subsequently, she would bemoan the fact that there was always a lot of *gaana* but never enough *khana.* "Everyday life was so difficult, how could we afford milk and *ghee*!" she would sigh.

If the conversation was about her years of *riyaz* with Guru Sawai Gandharva, she remembered the agony of having to manage three children plus a large extended family, go for her lessons to Kundagol, and also keep the hearth burning. "Very often six to seven of us have survived on a single loaf of bread …" she'd admit. Speaking of her guru, Gangubai would gush about the half-cup of *masala* milk he bought for her when he was in a good mood. "It was so delicious, spiked with *elaichi* and saffron …" Till her last days, she would speak of the Rs 75 she got for a programme in the early years, which barely made up for the train fare for Ramanna and herself, leaving behind little for the family, and even less for everyone's food.

Only when Gangubai Hangal became a musician in her own right and began to travel extensively for recordings and programmes did she start thinking about food positively. Food in her life always existed in comparison with the past. She could now afford to have two meals a day. She never gave up on her favourites, home-made *ghee* and home-made *chutney pudi*—her constant companions. There was so much innocence and simplicity in her imagination of food that it was hard to believe that someone could sound so upbeat about a cup of hot rice. She couldn't change even when she was exposed to the complicated world of musicians and their never-ending demands. Irrespective of the reality of her home, she could have commanded luxury in her professional career, but Gangubai was not charmed by any of this. On the contrary, she infused the modesty of her home in the world she inhabited.

"I would always tell the organizers to put me up in someone's house and not in a hotel. The host would come up to me and ask what I would like to eat. When I asked for a cup of hot rice and some curd, they would be shocked. I would relieve them by pulling out my bottle of *chutney pudi* and *ghee* from my bag … Soon they would stand before me holding out their palms, 'Gangubai, can we also taste some of the stuff in those bottles?'" she would recall with great pride. For a touch of the exotic, she always carried some *chuda* and *undi*, a small portion for herself and a large portion for the host. "I was famous for it, almost synonymous with *undi* and *chuda*," she would happily declare. '*Elli Gangu, undi chuda dabbi tegi* (Come on Gangu, open the packet of *chuda* and *undi*)'—Bhimu would say whenever we travelled together. Bismillah Khan was fond of them too." Bhimu would also, in advance, tell her to get enough *bhakri* (jowar roti) for him. Occasionally, when her desires were piqued, she would include *rasam* in her list of favourites.

When her career had begun to blossom, Gangubai brought her maternal uncle Ramanna and his family to live with her. Soon, the other maternal uncle's family also moved in with her. With an extended family of twenty-odd people, her aunts took over the kitchen, while Gangubai became the helper. She chopped, cleaned provisions, roasted, but was never the chief cook. Every musician who passed through Hubli–Dharwad had an open invitation to stop at Gangubai's house for a meal. With so many mouths to feed, so many kids going to school, this open-door hospitality was not easy on her. She probably could not even afford this, but it was something beyond economics. Gangubai would forgo a meal most willingly, but a visitor leaving her home without eating would make her unhappy.

Her speech was seldom loaded with the grand truths of life, she was a woman of right action. Often, it was her silence that did the talking. In her, one could see the spirit of communion—at once Hindu and Christian, as one finds it in *Sahana Bhavathu* or "Bless us, Lord, and these gifts which we are about to receive from Thy bounty. Through Christ our Lord. Amen." Both these prayers recited before eating invoke the ideals of love, compassion, charity and hospitality. Gangubai always whispered the name of Mylaralinga, the god of her prayers. Food, she seemed to believe, was a vehicle for spiritual transcendence.

My memory brims with the episodes that have taken place in all these years in Gangubai's house. Not once did she or her family treat me like a biographer who was there on "official" business. They drew me into their home and its warmth and never made me feel like an outsider. They took care of me as if I were their own.

After one visit, I was to leave for Bangalore by the night train. I had returned from an exhausting visit to Gangubai's childhood home in Shukravarapete, Dharwad. When I reached her present home it was past eight, with just two hours left for my train. Gangubai was sick with a fever, and nursing a hot pack. I sat beside her on the bed. She gave the hot bag to me and, turning her chest towards me, stretched herself on the bed like a little child, "*Madti* (Will you do it for me)?" Then she enquired about the state of her childhood home, "*Manige hogiddi* (Did you visit the house)?" No sooner had I begun describing the house to her than she suddenly asked, "*Neenu raatri gaadili hogtiyenu* (Are you leaving by the night train)?" Even before I could answer, Gangubai was out of bed and trudging towards the kitchen: "Lalitha, this girl has to eat now. Please get dinner ready for her." Lalithakka, who was already at it, was used to *ajji*'s anxieties, and nodded without turning towards her.

"Nobody takes me seriously," Gangubai mumbled, going up and down the narrow passage between her room and the kitchen. She looked at the timepiece on the wall, picked up her blouse which was on the pillow, and gave it to me: "Help me wear this." Soon after, she urged me to go have a wash and pack my bag, and feebly shouted from her room, "Is her dinner ready?"

Years later, barely four months after Gangubai's passing away, Babanna had done a repeat of this striking hospitality. Unexpectedly, there was trouble in Hubli and a curfew had been placed. My train was at two in the afternoon and no transport was available.

Babanna was getting worried. He said, "You have to leave at 12.30 even though the station is only ten minutes away. What if there is a problem?" A minute later he came back, "You eat on the train, let's not waste time having lunch at home," and went straight into the kitchen. Vaishnavi, his daughter who had come home for a vacation from Bombay, was making rice and that relieved Babanna. At that very moment his friend stepped in, exhausted by the long walk from his home due to the lack of public transport. Like every other visitor, his friend crossed the main hall, which was the museum, and came right into the kitchen. Babanna made him sit at the table, set a plate without a word, and served him the morning's *upma.* He kept a vessel on the other gas burner and made him tea. Afterward, Babanna sat at the table and got busy packing fruits and sweets for me. Vaishnavi packed my lunch, and we started for the station. "If there is trouble on the way and you feel hungry, have these fruits," Babanna advised. He was on tenterhooks until I reached the station. The train chugged out of Hubli station late that afternoon and, in about less than an hour, Babanna called. "All well with you? Did you eat the curd rice? Had it gone sour?"

After years of spending time with Gangubai's family, my memories of her have coalesced into a seamless whole, so much so that it is impossible for me to believe that Gangubai is dead. She is a living presence in me, so alive that to talk about her in the past tense triggers a strange ache. And how can she be gone—one sees her ways constantly in Babanna, Lalithakka and Manoj.

One evening, Gangubai had been discharged from the hospital, and as usual she was unwilling to eat or drink anything. "*Nanga agallo Babanna* (I can't, Babanna)," she pleaded with her son. "*Yaak traas kodtiya* (Why do you trouble me)?" Manoj screamed from the drawing room, and threatened to take her back to the hospital. The only thing that she really looked forward to was apple milkshake. She would drink it with great relish and click her tongue loudly. She would lift the steel tumbler and shake it till the last drop fell into her mouth. Even when she was very ill, she would manage to drink two to three sips of apple milkshake.

Walking back to Gangubai's home one of those evenings, I bought some apples for her. As usual, she had visitors. Once they had left, she gestured me to sit beside her. That was when I placed the bag of apples in her lap. She looked at them and her eyes lit up. Moving closer to me and beaming a smile, she whispered, "How do you know I like apples?" After that day, Gangubai would always ask me, "Have you brought apples for me?" It was our most private conversation.

Gangubai had gone back to the hospital. Manoj walked into the kitchen and went up to Lalithakka who was sitting on her wooden chair before the stove, waiting for the cooker to whistle the third time. "Is the lunch packed?" Manoj asked. "In five minutes …" she said, her gaze fixed on the pan on the neighbouring burner. Manoj tromped out and came back in less than a minute. The cooker had been turned off but Lalithakka sat there, just like before. "What's happening?" Manoj hollered. Lalithakka gave him a blank stare. "It is a hospital and there are timings. One cannot simply saunter in at convenience," Manoj screamed, words streaming out like missiles. "That old lady barely eats two spoons, and I want to send her rice as hot as possible. That is the only thing she has craved for all her life—hot rice with *ghee* …," Lalithakka screamed right back at Manoj.

Food was a medium for Gangubai through which she could step down from the pedestal of a legendary musician and initiate a conversation with people. During her last days, she began to be hospitalized very often. She was so tired of it all that she longed to get home. In the ICU, where visitors were restricted, she pushed her frail fingers into my hands and said, "I'm coming home early tomorrow morning, even before daybreak. Be there, don't go away. We can have tea together …"

Whenever she was in the hospital, she would talk glowingly of the *badi saunf* powder that was in a little box beside her pillow, as at her home. She would insist upon my having some of it, would drop a pinch of the powder into my palm. "How is it? Good, isn't it?" In this way, she would begin saying how it was made, who made it for her, how one should roast *saunf* and how much, how fine the powder has to be, that it was a good digestive—she would hold forth. Anyone who walked into the room had to have a taste of this, even the nurses weren't spared. "*Ajji*, you gave it to us yesterday," they would say. "*Hidi, hidi* …" she would insist that they stretch out their palms and, from there, would digress to talking of her Kannada teacher in school, who was from Mysore.

Ajji's frequent hospitalization made everyone anxious, She had become indecisive. Even when she had been seriously ill, everyone was sure of her recovery because of her enormous love of life. But in her last days, Gangubai was slowly giving up. Lalithakka would say, "She will be back in two days." But in her last days, Lalithakka was also suffering enormously from the thick cloud of uncertainty hanging in the air.

Despite longing for the past and being forced to straddle two worlds, there was enormous enthusiasm in Gangubai. But it was fading. She was withdrawing from her immediate surroundings, and this was very unlike her. The last time I visited Hubli before she passed away, I took *chutney pudi* and *undi* from my home. Lalithakka had packed some of that *chutney pudi* in her afternoon meal. When I went to the hospital that evening, she said, "*Nee chutney pudi tandyalla* (You brought *chutney pudi,* didn't you)?" She got breathless while speaking. After a few moments of rest, she said, "You made it with *dhal* ... I liked it …" Potamma, her nurse, later told me, how she had eaten one small *undi* throughout the day. She would keep a small portion in the corner of her mouth, allowing it to soak. When it was completely soft, she savoured it bit by bit.

Gangubai felt so completely satisfied with little things. Manoj told me of the day she had craved potato chips. He was so thrilled that his grandmother had finally asked for something. He quickly got on to his scooter, rushed to the market, bought a huge bag of fresh potato chips and placed it before her. She took precisely two pieces, and returned the bag to him saying, "I'm done. Give it to everyone." "Two! Did I go all the way to the market just for this? *Ajji*, take some more," he had said irritatedly. "I have seen such bad times, like the plague and the famine, when people died of deprivation and starvation. Just because I can afford to buy a bag of chips, must I eat more than my share? I have had my fill. Give it to the others."

Gangubai would quote Gandhiji, "Food is for sustaining the body." She lived most of her life in a state of self-denial, never fully able to accept the abundance of food. Her excessive concerns about food spilled into her ethical practice of hospitality.

Historically, food and eating practices in India have been important indicators of caste identity. Eating practices are instrumental both in constructing those identities and negotiating their meaning. Curiously, while Gangubai belonged to the Gangamath caste, a meat-eating community, her eating practices were extremely Brahminical. Except for the use of garlic, cooking meat in their kitchen was a rarity. "Who could tell my mother was not a Brahmin?" Gangubai would say rather proudly. "We lived in a Brahmin colony and even the Brahmins told my mother that she was more Brahmin than all of them ..." Ambabai was an extremely religious person and even dressed like Brahmin women.

* * *

Gangubai looked forward to the Kundagol music festival conducted in memory of her guru every year. In her late years, when she had lost the mobility of her younger days, she would sit in the open space between the stage and the dining hall. For the three days during the festival, the kitchen fire is never put off: lunch, dinner, and tea are served through the day and night without break. Hundreds of volunteers attend to the non-stop flow of guests. Even when she was pushing ninety-five, Gangubai would watch all this with an eagle eye. *Oota maadidyenu* (Have you eaten)?" she would ask everybody who passed by. "But I did not see you come from the dining hall," she would say. "You must eat the *huggi*, it's made in memory of my guru, *gurugala prasada*," Gangubai would urge them to have the sweet dish made from broken wheat, jaggery and coconut. For this overwhelming hospitality she did not have to know them personally. Each person who stepped into the *pandal* was her own.

* * *

Food discourses are integral to the ways in which individuals and cultures identify themselves. Communities, even localities, set themselves apart through "taste". Gangubai's requirements were modest and minimal—was this her language of protest, a rejection of intolerable social constraints? Was her largesse, then, a metaphor of compliance? Our bodies are products of history, emblems of the practices and attitudes we have inherited as part of our culture. Till her end, Gangubai stuck on to her past. Like Gandhiji, she did everything—washing, cleaning, shopping, cooking and carrying firewood—right till the end.

The mythical significance of food in her household came from what our ancestors believed—it had to be consumed in communion, in affection, and as a gift from the gods. It was a field uncorrupted, free from the snares of society and far from the logic of rational debates. According to Gangubai's philosophy of food, it allowed for the self-consciousness of humanity and, being more than fuel for the body, was a moral and spiritual challenge.

The song of her soul

Gangubai's simplicity was always misleading. Her articulation was uncluttered and plain, but it more often than not pointed to something very profound. In an interview she once said:

> Music is an art. It is so both for listeners and the performer. In the first place, the musician tries to present his form. Once the boundaries of the physical are crossed by the artiste and the audience, there remains no difference between the singer and the listener—the passage of experience is the same for both. To relish Hindustani music, there is no need to be knowledgeable about the musical form. All you need is a good heart and a sharp mind. Both of these belong to the experiential realm. Knowledge helps, but also disturbs. I have seen enlightened audiences carrying out dry discussions on the subtleties of a raga or a form. But in an intuitive listener, the experience can be far deeper, beyond the grasp of the mere listener.

Her explanation is the core of the philosophy of Indian music, according to which the musician must primarily activate her inner source and plumb its depths. Hence, traditionally, the Hindustani musician underwent rigorous training, which endowed her with incredible skill and control. In fact, Gangubai's words echo the words of eminent musicologist Sheila Dhar in her essay, "The Raga: An Inward Journey". The central object of a classical musician's labour, she says, is not the cultivation of a beautiful tone, but the development of an almost limitless capability in articulation.

> The physical sound of the music is, in ideal circumstances, only a medium and not the end product. To the connoisseur, a voice is only as beautiful as what it conveys. The physical body of the music is to the musician what a writing tool is to the poet. The listener is trained to tune into the highly charged state of consciousness of the performer rather than to the physical condition of the sound that carries the music.

Hence, for the initiated listener, truth lies in the experience and not in the beauty of a voice.

After a tonsillitis operation in her early youth, Gangubai's mellifluous, silken voice underwent a dramatic change: there was not much euphony left in her voice. It became throaty and masculine. Her broad, base voice, strong with androgynous power was not easily manoeuvrable. But it did not bother Gangubai. When people noticed *mardangi* (maleness) of her voice, she would say, "the way I sing with strength is a question of style not of gender." With a voice that was by no stretch of imagination "sweet", people often referred to her as "Gangubua" like they addressed male musicians. This appellation indicated the popular impression that there was nothing feminine about her music, but it never annoyed her. She would belt out a hearty laugh. Music was her purpose, the voice was a mere medium—of this she was never in doubt.

Nevertheless, her voice did become the focus of discussion and continues to remain so. Most critics who wrote about Gangubai's music could hardly resist the temptation of making a comment about her voice. Contemporary and younger generation musicians succumbed to this enticement as well—not surprising, considering the resounding power that her voice exuded. But what they all universally agreed to was the purity of her music. "Her voice is strong, not syrupy. It does not appeal to sweetness at all," senior critic Raghava Menon remarked in his book *Indian Music.* He compared her baritone timbre to the church bell—strong and chaste, resonant and carrying. Eventually, what emerged from her music was a noble passion and supreme strength of character. Voice did become, at the end of the recital, a trivial issue for the listener as well.

If voice was an index of a musicians merit, there were other deeper indices to perceive one's musical persona. The *shadja* (the meaning born out of six notes) is the nucleus of a raga. The musician, with immense concentration and intensity, awakens the *shadja* before he begins to explore other melodic patterns of the raga. Gangubai's voice was not the kind that soared three octaves effortlessly. However, between the lower *shadja* and the upper *shadja* she painted a picture of totality. She shut her eyes to the world in a manner in which music became a meditation, urging her into its depths. The contemplative seeking would gradually unfold into a luminous journey, as she rigorously unravelled the notes and its microtones. Interestingly, a lot has been written and said about how musicians treat their *shadja.* The character of their music is largely determined by their treatment of this fixed (*sthayi*) note. Abdul Karim Khan's *shadja* had an enchanting mesmeric quality following from his penchant for the purity of the note. Bhimsen Joshi's *shadja* bore resemblance to Kesarbai Kerkar's *shadja* of bold and emotive resonances. The poet Bendre often made observations about Gangubai's and Krishna's treatments of the *shadja*, and could even make fascinating distinctions between the overall personalities of their music.

True to the Kirana stamp, Gangubai was also a pursuer of the *sur.* For her, tradition was of immense value. She would say, "It is the labour of one who teaches and the one who learns." When the air of change and novelty was blowing across the entire country, it was only Gangubai and Hirabai Badodekar, who dared to stand up to convention. Tradition, for Gangubai (or Hirabai) was not conservatism, but a deep reverence for the knowledge that was passed on by the guru, a belief that it was complete. New depths had to be found within the framework of tradition itself, and never outside of it. Faith in the guru and her art was above everything else for Gangubai, hence she never had to battle with the effects of increasing commercialization of music. Her propriety reflected in her music as well: her voice was unique because of her *sadhana*, and she never found the need to introduce any frills in her music. She sang the truth, as it stood before her, and that was Gangubai's virtuosity. Her music and her persona were never two different things: one was always the extension of the other.

Like her guru, she had a voice that was not very compliant: the initial minutes of a performance were always a raging battle between body and spirit, but she was not one to be cowed down. She battled with it out in the open, for all to see, and drew everyone into her solid music—a music that was the picture of a deep inner struggle and a flawless devotion.

Gangubai's performances were engrossing, but there were several occasions when her mind would not cope with her spirit. A Bhairav rendition at the Sawai Gandharva Festival, Pune, perhaps in the 1990s, just refused to take flight much as she tried. A voice that had gone as stiff as starch, and an imagination that simply refused to find a language, left her rendition dry and listless. But Gangubai held on for a good fifty minutes, trying to coax it with her solid faith, and what followed was a moving Hindol. Music, like her life, was a constant tussle between several odds: winning and losing were not her destination points. She toiled with resilience. In her case, music was never a spectacle raised above life—it was rooted in mortal struggles.

The Abdul Karim Khan school of the Kirana *gharana* emphasized more on melody and less on rhythm. In the true spirit of the founder of the *gharana*, Sawai Gandharva and all his students—Bhimsen Joshi, Gangubai Hangal and Firoze Dastur—sang with their soul. It became impossible for any musician of post-Independence India to resist the charm of these musicians. Abdul Karim Khan saab never indulged in complicated *taan* patterns. Instead, his *alaap* was long and contemplative. But a close study of his lineage reveals that, except for Bhimsen Joshi and Roshanara Begum, no other practitioner of the *gharana* employed complex *taan* patterns. An old recording of Roshanara Begum's rendition of *Jaunpuri* is a case in point. Richly imaginative, her *alaap* is mellifluous, her *boltaan*s and *murki*s are sharp and nuanced. The details she works out in her *taan*s are amazing. You can't help notice that many of Roshanara's inflections are Bhimsen Joshi's too. The short, stunning rendition of *Shuddha Kedar*, "*Sawan Ki Boondaniyan*", captures the genius of Bhimsen Joshi completely. His long, breathtaking *taan*s are replete with complex combinations of *swara*s. While Bhimsen Joshi hunts down the notes, Roshanara unleashes her *taan*s with a quiet toughness. If the former's rendition is torrential, the latter's is serene. Yet, both are deep and touching.

Gangubai was, perhaps, a quintessential practitioner of the Kirana. Firoze Dastur also largely adhered to the practices and style of the Kirana, but Gangubai's music was austere. If Bhimsen Joshi's music was marked by wild passion and Roshanara's with profound emotion and complexity, Gangubai's music was ascetic. She adhered to the *gharana* tradition marked by slow tempo and the gradual unfolding of the ragas. Each note was a melodic idea, and it was elongated in a manner that evoked tranquility. This is perhaps why the treatment of the *shadja* is so crucial to the Kirana practitioners. It seems as if the spirit of the musician merges with the spirit of the note.

The Kirana note is very delicate and tender, it captures the subtlest shades of tone. Abdul Wahid Khan, if one could call him the co-founder of the Kirana, sang with a full-throated voice and never missed the Kirana mark. Bhimsen Joshi's voice may have been the earthy, full-bodied kind, but it still didn't possess the timbre of Abdul Karim Khan, Sawai Gandharva or Firoze Dastur's voice. After the change in her voice, the string-like and remarkable flexibility had been replaced by a full-throatedness. When a pioneer like Abdul Karim Khan made his *alaapi*-oriented, nuanced style the special forte of Kirana, how could Gangubai achieve the Kirana style with her strapping voice? Gangubai's hearty expression did not even demonstrate the tonal control that Bhimsen Joshi was capable of. However, the Kirana expression never suffered because of her voice.

Even when one is a strong adherent of tradition, one rarely finds a student who is a carbon copy of his guru. The guru's thoughts and ideas pass through the student's creative process, and synthesize into an independent creation. So, even as the *gharana* tradition remains inviolate, new musical possibilities integrate in a new artiste. Tradition combines with innovation. One can observe these features in ragas that are sung by the Kirana practitioners. Take, for instance, how Gangubai, who is a monument of style and technique, carves exquisite glides as she descends into the *mandra* through the notes *sa* and *dha* while rendering *Shuddha Kalyan.* In the case of *Pooriya Dhanashree*, her repeated enunciation of the *swara*-cluster *ni re ga ma—ma pa—dha pa—ma ga re sa* for the celebrated *bandish* "*Ab To Rutuman*" scales new emotional heights each time. When Gangubai engaged in repetition, an extraordinary intensity of musical expression was produced. Her prayerful renditions with long *meend* phrases and extraordinary *taan*s had a sustained tension. Her singing neither had the magnificence of Sawai Gandharva nor the brilliance of Bhimsen Joshi, yet it had a spiritual edge. Like Roshanara, Gangubai also performed *gamak taan*s. However, the manner in which she developed a raga lacked the lyricism of her Kirana predecessors: Gangubai carved a style of her own.

Any sensitive artiste expounds her style with an abiding classicism, exploring her musical ideology and the structure of her art based on the individual quality of her voice. The sharp and intuitive Gangubai had a remarkable sense of voice and temperament, an innate aesthetic sense, and sensitivity to the usefulness of notes and phrases. Particular musical idioms suit only particular voices, so a musician usually absorbs and adapts what suits her voice and rejects the rest. Gangubai was never out of depth with any raga and was perceptive about what suited her voice, and what it was capable of. She was a musician who had a profound understanding of the raga and knew its movement, its high point, its climaxes, and how to create tensions. In his essay on the Kirana *gharana,* Kumar Prasad Mukherji recalls an anecdote from 1943, from a private concert in Calcutta. Gangubai was a young musician of thirty. She had sung *Lalit* with an elaborate *vistar* and several well-structured *taan*s. She eshchewed all the *taan*s that followed in *Bilaskhani Todi*, and is said to have remarked, *Is raag ki bhavna main taan ki jagah nahin hai.* Mukherji confesses that he is able to realize the wisdom of her statement only later in life. Just as Gangubai understood the nature of ragas, she understood the limitations of her voice too. Though she maintained her distance from lighter forms of music saying that all the music her guru taught her was devotional, it could well be true that she gave these up because her voice changed. A loud, heavy voice that lacked flexibility couldn't do justice to the delicate, nuanced nature of *thumri* or Bhakti music. She eventually reckoned that her voice was best suited for classical music alone. Whenever faced with the question, she would say, "I do not deny that a musician has to make compromises for the sake of her listeners. I myself, at the beginning of my career, sang every form of semi-classical music, except the *ghazal.* Having given these up, I do sometimes sing the raga of my listener's choice." During her early years as a concert artiste, there were apprehensions about her voice. "It teased their notion of the feminine," she would say. "Voice was a mere vehicle for me. Music was my prayer. I closed my eyes and sang. Little else mattered."

If Kumar Gandharva refashioned his music to suit his single-lung power, Gangubai's was no mean achievement either. She quietly reworked a voice that had transformed from mellifluous to manly. Kumar Gandharva's music was marked by a restless search, enigmatic and mystifying. Gangubai's music was intense and introspective. It was bold: there was no place in it for meek moaning. Marked by anguish, her music was chaste, and shorn of flamboyant airs.

Sweetness is a quality that is associated with most female singers. Uncharged by the power of *riyaz*, sweetness alone cannot take an individual's music very far. This power, which in music parlance is called *vazan,* is considered very important. Gangubai's voice had no sweetness, but fortified by exacting *sadhana*, her voice had enormous power—sometimes it almost seemed that it consisted of a protest of her woes, a cutting pathos. Though she was a pious adherent of a tradition, this never translated into arrogant self-gratification that robbed her art of its virtue.

The progress of an artist is a process of continual self-sacrifice, a continuous negation of the self and surrendering to the moment.

Music, she knew, could never be a prepared exercise, particularly for a seeker. It was a process that unfurled in uncalculated moments, acquiring a breath and movement of its own. While she was conscious of the complex nature of this highly intuitive art, she was honest to admit to its flip side as well. "There were times I could never submit to my music, much as I wanted to. The unending problems of my life would crush me. I have felt like putting down my tanpura and fleeing … but then, I had promises to keep, to my music and to my life. Nothing was ever easy for me …" she would say. Her intonation and articulation brought people under a spell and even the shortcomings of her style and voice were ignored. The Kirana *gharana*, as musicologists recognize, was born out of a deep urge for self-expression. Its music, therefore, emerges from a large canvas of silence. It is marked by restraint and contemplation. Gangubai's music is a case in point.

Gangubai often faced the criticism that she paid little attention to literary content. When she sang, the lyrics of the *bandish* became incoherent and dissolved into the flow of her music. Since most of her contemporaries and *gurubandhu*s sang *thumri, natyasangeet* and devotional music, they were more sensitive to lyrics. Hence, Gangubai's irreverence to words became conspicuous. The "word" in most compositions in classical music renounces its literary function and follows the laws of music. This liberates words from their singularity of purpose and bestows upon them eternal possibilities as they unite with notes and musical ideas. The word in her music attained a higher significance. Breaking free from the shackles of the word and its meaning, Gangubai was intensely engaged in the pursuit of artistic expression, seeking the infinite shades of meaning that surpassed the grasp of literary language. Gangubai's *Marwa* matches the towering rendition of Ustad Amir Khan, where the eponymous words of the *bandish "Suno Suno Batiya"* become the landing point, while the rest of the composition becomes incidental. *Maane Sakhi Mora Kanha*, a 1969 *Madhuvanti* rendition breaks free from all earthly tethers and soars heavenwards. In this particular performance her voice is not very fluid, like in her

Komal Rishabh Asavari of the early 1960s. Her rugged, obdurate voice evokes two ends of the spectrum at once—a soulful evocation of grassroot emotions and an uplifting sublime appeal. Krishna, as the remarkable support, holds on to the poetry of the words even in her long, effortless passages, but Gangubai lets herself go and doggedly chases the notes, painting a picture of longing and despair.

The presentation of the *bandish* not only indicates the various notes of the raga and their internal relationships, but also how exactly they behave within the context of the raga. Gangubai's heavy voice with a viscous texture lacked felicity, and hence she chose to express herself in slow *taan*s and *gamaks*. But there were times when her musical aspirations defied her own voice. One would think that for a broad, base voice, ragas that operate in *mandra* and *madhya sapthak*s are best suited, but Gangubai has demonstrated great emotional potential in the upper octaves. Her short rendition of *Chandrakauns*, a recording from the 1960s, *Kab Ghar Aayo Piya*, is touching. The spacious *alaap*, full of *meends* and emotive passages, is haunting. Incidentally, she is not accompanied by Krishna in this rendition. In *Basant* and *Maluha Kedar*, she delivers breathtaking cascading *taan*s, quite contrary to the nature of her voice. One also witnesses moments of failed judgements—permutations and combinations that collapse miserably—but that is due to a stubborn, disobedient voice, and not because she failed in her understanding of the raga. However, you can see Bhimsen Joshi making these wrong moves too. Many a time, he implants certain *taan* patterns of *Shuddha Kalyan* into *Marwa* or *Abhogi* and it turns out to be an aesthetic disaster. In Gangubai, you will never find such transgressions. While her delineation remains valiant, she never dared to take the imaginative flights Bhimsen Joshi did. She was a musician of great poise and spaciousness, who added masculine vigour to the regal grace of Kirana.

Listening to all the Kirana maestros in a row—beginning with Abdul Karim Khan and Abdul Wahid Khan to Hirabai Badodekar to Sawai Gandharva to his famous disciples, one cannot but be amazed at the dynamism of this music school. In this regard, musicologist

Vamanrao Deshpande observes in *Between Two Tanpuras*: "Each generation imported new ideas and yet the characteristics of the *gharana* remained inviolate."

Abdul Karim Khan spent his entire lifetime on perfecting the note and its microtonal existence. There is a lovely anecdote that illustrates his obsession. He is believed to have practised only two ragas—*Todi* and *Darbari*, One day, his cousin Wahid Khan, unable to contain his curiosity, asked him: "Why do you always sing only these two ragas?" To this Karim Khan answered, "If the sun didn't set, I would have practised just *Todi.* But unfortunately it does, and so I switch to *Darbari.* One lifetime is insufficient to master a raga." Abdul Karim Khan was a perfectionist who would get carried away by the beauty of the note and its position. He valued the note more highly than the discipline of the *gharana.* Sawai Gandharva's music had a lot of intellectual content in it. His *taan*s indicate a clear departure from his gurus. He was more organized, and concentrated on the architecture of his presentation. It just wasn't in him to feel contented with the usual formulations of the Kirana.

Bhimsen Joshi, like his guru, made his presentation rhythm-oriented, so much so that he even tailored his *vilambit* portions suitably. That explains why he was the only Kirana practitioner who preferred *ektaal* and *vilambit teentaal.* Gangubai's style was a clear departure from all this. All the Kirana maestros shared the same value system, but the manner in which they articulated it depended on their personalities. It manifested in different ways—restraint, silence, understatement and gesture scored over physical completeness. The music of each of the Kirana singers is a clear reflection of an original, highly individual personality, and not a mindless stereotype. In essence, they capture the core of the Indian *guru-shishya parampara,* not just of music, but all disciplines of art. All learning involves vision. And what the guru transfers to the disciple, in this case, is his "entire inner musical self", making it spiritual in character. The interaction, experience, the "said" and the "unsaid" leave lasting imprints on the collective pool of *the gharana*'s wealth.

According to Sheila Dhar in *Raga 'n Josh,* the raga performance is an evocation that aspires to break free of time, by itself becoming a kind of time. Music, for Gangubai, was an expression of faith and the note had to be searched and discovered each time a phrase was attempted. Hence, there was no definite or exact position for the note. The melodic leaps and subtle oscillations in pitch that she achieves in *Abhogi* are brilliant. In her case, a penetrating search for the note was more important than ornamentation. She could never achieve the sweetness, smoothness or the delicate artistry of tones that the Kirana was noted for, but with inherited talent, scrupulous cultivation and years of struggle what she achieved was unbelievable.

It is a myth that great music rides on a great voice. Gangubai disproved it every living moment of her life. Indian classical music is neither a perfect piece of poetry nor a premeditated symphony. It does not have a definite aesthetic ambition. It takes birth and develops at the given moment along the shore of tradition. Gangubai's music was a celebration of such imperfections.

Krishna

After years of frequent visits to Gangubai's house, I could slowly see a picture emerge. The picture was tossed between shades of grey with bursts of bright gold intermittent. There was an underlying mood of sadness, of suppression, sacrifice and denial.

Great lines of poetry will not reduce suffering. Great music, like deep friendship and intense works of literature, is never free from agony. A lasting friendship is not a castle built in thin air. It is often built on a foundation of remarkable selflessness and unconditional love. Only piety and unwavering abstinence can keep it tenacious. To deny its weak, vulnerable moments would be to deify it.

The struggles of Krishna, Gangubai's first child, contained all these moments. It was sheer nobility that helped her rise above natural human desires and commit herself to a life of intense dedication.

As the picture on the canvas begins to sharpen, the saddest strain emerges from Krishna. Krishna was also responsible for what happened to her, but Gangubai had a role to play in it—that makes it all the more sadder. But this is something Gangubai never admitted to. Krishna's life was poignant, but one could not help being moved by Gangubai's plight as well.

Krishna was the eldest of Gangubai's three children. She was born in 1929, when Gangubai herself was still a child of sixteen. She was born before they moved to Hubli from their Kamanakatte home in Dharwad. Gangubai would put her little Kitty in the cloth cradle, and sit beside, rocking it with her left hand. The tanpura sat firmly on her right lap and, as she rocked Krishna to sleep, she tried holding on to the elusive musical note—trapped between motherhood and music. Krishna was a weak child. Gangubai was so anxious a mother that she never left Krishna alone even for a minute. She constantly carried her around. The little Krishna cried of a stomach ache every now and then and, rather horrifyingly, this reminded Gangubai of her mother Ambabai, who had frequent bouts of similar pain before she finally succumbed to them.

Mallikarjun Mansur, who was back at the drama company, invariably visited them in the afternoons. "*Tangi*, you go finish whatever work you have, I will sit by her cradle," he would say to Gangubai. If Krishna was asleep, he curled up beside the cradle and took his siesta. If she was awake, he rocked her cradle, hummed a song or two and played with her. Meanwhile Gangubai attended to all the household chores.

For most of her concert tours, the infant Krishna went along with Gangubai. She would either be left with Ramanna or someone else backstage. Many a time Krishna wailed, but Gangubai could not attend to her. "I offered myself to the god of my heart, and left her to the god of this world," she would say, recalling those trying moments. Krishna got better as she grew up, and her childhood illness troubled her less often. But Gangubai rarely left her behind.

Accompanying Gangubai on her musical tours influenced Krishna: she not only got to listen to a lot of her mother's music, but also to a whole lot of other musicians. Krishna, who was extremely sharp and receptive like Gangubai in her childhood, was like a sponge, which instantly absorbed everything. Her grasping power was amazing, she could reproduce whatever she heard without having to struggle over it. In fact, the little Krishna started imitating her mother and was capable of closely replicating Gangubai, almost like a photocopier machine.

Krishna's voice was fluent, fluid and remarkably felicitous. It could ply the three octaves with ease and could negotiate complex musical phrases effortlessly. Over the years, Gangubai began to trust Krishna's musical instincts. Since Krishna anyway went along with her, she began to play the tanpura for Gangubai. To begin with, Gangubai gave her an occasional phrase or two and later, she gave her small opportunities for *saath.*

The house was always flowing over with musicians—Bhimsen Joshi, Kagalkar Bua, Dattopant Desai, Mallikarjun Mansur, Basavaraj Rajguru, Hirabai, Siddheshwari Devi, Gangubai's trusted accompanists, or fellow musicians from Hubli and Dharwad. The house was full of music when Guru Sawai Gandharva stayed with Gangubai, and there would be engaging discussions on the life and work of musicians. Krishna was the biggest beneficiary of all this. The boys were interested, but only fleetingly.

Curiously, Gangubai never trained Krishna formally. Krishna's learning was intuitive and by observation. It's surprising that Krishna never demanded or aspired to a formal music education. By the time she was in her late teens, Krishna knew all the ragas from Gangubai's repertoire and practised them on her own. Gangubai asked her to do *kharaj riyaz*—holding the notes in the lower octave, which is believed to be the sure route to achieving perfection of pitch and pliability—but Krishna never did enough of it. This was something Gangubai did in all her learning years with great rigour.

Krishna's early renditions—sung with Bhimsen Joshi when AIR Dharwad was inaugurated in 1950, and later during the unification of what became the state of Karnataka—are a connoisseur's delight. Her crystal clear voice, rich in emotive quality, soars in splendour, and she is a competent match to the fluid prowess of Bhimsen Joshi. Together, they sang Bendre's poem "*Onde Onde Karnataka Onde*" and Huyilgol Narayan Rao's "*Udayavaagali Namma Cheluva Kannada Naadu*".

From the early 1960s, Krishna became Gangubai's acknowledged accompanist. If Babanna became her manager for worldly dealings, Krishna became her music manager. She followed her mother like a shadow: she was always there, but never on her own.

Soon, Gangubai delegated the task of planning her concerts to Krishna. Krishna was extremely meticulous and maintained a diary with detailed notes of all their concerts, with their date, place, time and venue, and the ragas sung. She even made a note of the *bandish*es they sang at every concert. So when they set out for their next concert, Krishna would throw up a concert plan and Gangubai, who was such a stickler for perfection, more or less agreed with it. Sometimes, she would suggest minor changes. Krishna was in step with Gangubai's thinking and rarely misjudged what her mother would want them to sing at a particular concert. In later years, Krishna even kept track of the saris her mother and she wore, and made sure that they didn't repeat themselves at the next concert. Both Gangubai and Krishna had a simple dressing taste, and at their most elaborate would wear a string of pearls.

Krishna was a major helping hand at home as well—she was dutifully engaged in cleaning, cooking, organizing, and going to the market. She was also extremely fond of the kids. When Babu's and Narayan's kids were born, Krishna doted on them. The kids loved their aunt. Like Babanna and Nani, they too began to call her Kittakka and came running to her for every little thing. When Krishna was around, nobody could raise their voice against them. The children knew this well and often used her as a shield, even from their grandmother.

When the kids started going to school, they got a new set of uniforms and a new set of books—no hand-me-downs, insisted Krishna. It was difficult to make ends meet with their shoestring budget, but, when it came to the kids, they made no compromise. Gangubai completely approved of this, she would make sure she kept money aside for uniforms and books. Just before school began, Gangubai and Krishna would sit down to wrap the books with brown paper. "Kittakka, wake us up at five in the morning … We have to revise …" the children would say before they went to bed. "Oh yes, I will," she would assure them. But the next morning, the children would be so disappointed with their aunt. She would wake them up only at 6.30 a.m. "See … you have the whole day at your disposal. Why should you get up at five? I will see to it that no one disturbs you through the day," she would reason with them.

Krishna was particular about everything: even about whom she bought vegetables from, or what grocery was bought at which store. There was a particular shop from where she bought red chillies. At the far end of the market sat an old lady who sold fresh greens, only she could be trusted. For tamarind she went to her good old trusted store in another bylane of the market. And for the *undi* and *avalakki* made for the kids, for which only the best ingredients could be bought, she, along with her mother, walked an extra mile to buy the stuff. Krishna was very orderly, house-proud and neat.

Susheela Ambike would recall how Kitty faithfully made a trip to the market each time they came to Delhi for concerts. Gangubai was not particular, as it is clear from the Hangal Pant Company episode. She had to buy things for the children and her concern ended there. Gangubai never had the patience to individually choose pieces for each of them. After Krishna started doing all the shopping, Gangubai would not even step out. She would stay at home and perhaps read a book.

Kitty's favourite shopping place was Karol Bagh, where she would flit from one cart to the other. "I used to wonder why she collected so many things!" Susheela had remembered. "Mausi, it will fit someone or the other"—this was Krishna's rationale. Both Gangubai and Krishna shopped for everybody else and never for themselves. They received such joy in giving and sharing that they never wanted anything in return.

"Each time they went to Calcutta, my mother-in-law would tell Krishna to buy two–three sets of clothes for every child because the rates were cheap there. They would choose the right size, but it would all be of the same colour and the same print," Lalitha remembers. "In all these years and so many trips, I have rarely seen my mother-in-law and Krishna spending on themselves."

Krishna's nature combined characteristics of both her mother and grandmother. She was god-fearing like her grandmother, and penned songs and composed like her. She acquired her selfless nature and innate goodness from Gangubai. And like Gangubai, she had a tremendous strength to suppress her innermost feelings and desires.

Constitutionally, Krishna was very weak. Even though she recovered from the agony she went through in her childhood, it resurfaced every now and then and troubled her. When Gangubai and Krishna had gone to Baroda for a performance, Dr Ambegaonkar invited them for lunch. It was a multiple-course meal, with an entire spread of fried food. The doctor, a caring host, made sure all his guests were comfortable and politely enquired with each of them if they were satisfied. "Why aren't you eating any *pakora*s, Krishna? All the other guests seem to love them," he asked affectionately. Krishna timidly looked at her mother for help, and Gangubai told him of Krishna's sensitive stomach. She had to keep away from rich food. "You have to bring her to my clinic tomorrow," he insisted.

The next day, Dr Ambegaonkar did a thorough examination and discovered that Krishna had appendicitis and advised emergency surgery. He explained her condition to Gangubai and advised her to get Krishna treated as soon as they reached Hubli. Upon returning, Gangubai did nothing about it. In fact, she chose to remain very quiet about it all. It was bothering Krishna, but she was not the kind to express anything. She bore it silently as long as she could. Krishna's condition began to worsen, and she could no longer suffer in silence. Only then did Gangubai rush her to the trusted Dr Joshi who said a surgery was imperative. "It is an emergency," he said emphatically, and tersely added that they were very late. It became clear later that it was Gangubai's fear of surgery that had made her postpone it endlessly. Krishna went through the surgery, while Gangubai occupied some dark shadowy corner of the hospital nervously. The operation was a success and Krishna began to recover well. Gangubai, who was gripped by fear until then, slowly emerged out of her shell. Krishna's fluctuating health was a matter of immense concern to Gangubai.

Even after Babu and Narayan were married, when Gangubai showed no signs of getting Krishna married, people asked her questions. She used to tell them: Krishna may not be able to cope with the responsibilities of marriage and motherhood. "I do not want her to get married and suffer," she would say, and more or less put an end to the conversation. Also, what if she was not allowed to sing? These things worried her and hence Gangubai never made a serious attempt to get Krishna married. Gangubai always took unilateral decisions about Krishna, and hardly consulted her in the process.

With the passing years, Krishna's growing confidence in her music was perceivable. She came into her own: a mellifluous performer, who had a quiet, inner restlessness in her music, as opposed to Gangubai's deeply devout rendering. When Siddeshwari Devi was in her last days, Gangubai and Krishna went to visit the ailing musician. "If there is anything that we can do for you, please let us know," Krishna had said holding her hand with immense regard. "Darling, I'm dying. What could comfort me but some soulful music? Will you sing Bhairavi for me?" Siddeshwari Devi requested. Krishna sat by her side and sang Bhairavi. After listening to Krishna's rendition, Siddeshwari had wept. "God bless you, dear," she had said, drawing Krishna close.

Krishna became a vital aspect of Gangubai's music concerts. Gangubai presented the *alaap*, while Krishna joined her in the *bandish.* If Gangubai made a statement, Krishna interpreted it. If she presented a *meend taan*, it was followed by a *gamak taan.* Gangubai used to carve a solid picture of bold strokes in the lower octaves, and Krishna would effortlessly leap into the higher octaves, gripping the listener with every single note. Krishna's understanding of her mother's music was so implicit that whatever she sang was in sync with Gangubai's *manodharma.* She was extremely imaginative, but she never tried to turn a concert in her direction. If Gangubai's music was filled with dedication, Krishna's was poignant. Gangubai herself got swayed by Krishna's touches on many occasions. For instance, in an early Doordarshan recording in the black-and-white era, Gangubai sings *Mero Mann Bandh* in Yaman. Krishna's flourishes are so beautiful and subtle that an enraptured Gangubai nods in appreciation. When Krishna touched the *shadja*, it was hard not to lose one's soul over it. The note was so plaintive and had such rich resonances that it shook the inner recesses of one's soul. Gangubai was stately, Krishna was a picture of poise. In music circles, Krishna was called *antara*—the latter half of a *bandish* that soars into higher realms. She had the capability to elevate a concert, and she did it quietly—just like the shadow that lengthens behind you as the day progresses. Bendre had remarked more than once that Krishna was Gangubai's soul.

Vijaya Mulay, an officer with the Censor Board, who made a documentary on Gangubai in the 1980s, asked her to present a new *bandish* for the film. "Krishna used to be so quick. She immediately told her mother, 'Akka, you will by force of habit go back to singing what we normally do in *Miyan ki Todi.* Let's sing *Langar Ka Kariye* in *drut.* Don't forget.' Krishna was wonderful," Mulay narrated. Krishna was a guide, and a personal reminder—Gangubai was completely dependent on her.

Gangubai was a caring teacher, even though with her hectic schedule she could train very few. She was very concerned about the progress of her students. If, in the previous class they had not been able to achieve something, she would see to it that this was addressed in the next class. Every class, there would be something new for the students, something unusual. She taught them exactly the way her guru had taught her. She would be exacting as well. She would teach a single raga for three years. Once, one of her students, Ashok Nadiger, asked her if he could introduce the *pancham* note, which is omitted in the variety of Raga Bageshree that Gangubai advocated. "No, if you want to sing like the others, why learn from me?" she had said brusquely.

She had little patience for those who put in little effort. Gangubai walked out of the room if she felt the student was not doing his best. Kittakka, who would be lingering around, would step in quietly and first comfort the student. Then she would demonstrate the technique with great patience. She was absolutely wonderful—if Gangubai had taught the *vistar* (the broad outline of a raga), she filled in the details. She could play all the *theka*s on the tabla. So when there was no *tabaliya* for the students, she sat there providing them with the *saath.*

Gangubai used to think a lot about her music. All her sleeping and waking hours, even while she was at something else—music consumed her. Krishna was unlike Gangubai. According to Gangubai's students, Krishna was an "instant mix" and could produce brilliant sparks spontaneously. Nevertheless, there were times when she outdid herself. Once, for the Malhar festival, she had to sing four variants of *Malhar.* She knew *Miyan ki Malhar, Megh Malhar* and *Nat Malhar.* For the fourth, she looked through the books, learnt of a *Jayant Malhar*, and worked on it. She made extensive notes and practised just that the next two–three days. If she made up her mind to do something, she worked very hard for it. Krishna, a talented composer, has composed over four hundred songs, whereas Gangubai didn't compose even one. Krishna needed creative outlets, whereas Gangubai was happy being a firm upholder of tradition, and all her creative energies were invested within it.

Krishna was such an understanding accompanist that Gangubai had to just begin the concert and Krishna knew exactly what the structure of the concert would be. She had a clear idea of the build-up her mother was trying to achieve. The reason for this understanding was also probably because of the very little age difference between them. Since most of her learning was untutored, Krishna could never explain her music theoretically. If asked for the notation, she would say, "I don't know. For that, you will have to ask my mother. I can only demonstrate it for you."

With age catching up on Gangubai, and Krishna becoming a very attractive part of her concert, organizers began to approach Krishna. Gangubai was a legend: solid and robust. She was still a big favourite with listeners for the austerity in her music. Krishna, more than providing *saath* had now become her co-singer. A major portion of the concert was handled by Krishna. Neither Krishna nor Babanna, however, took any decisions of their own. And hence, all requests had to be routed through Gangubai. "You invite me, and I will bring Krishna along. You will get to hear a good deal of her music," Gangubai would convince the organizers. This practice continued for many years: each time someone came asking for Krishna, they got the same answer. Gradually, over the years, everyone in the music circles understood that Gangubai denied Krishna an independent existence and stopped making these requests.

There were two reasons for this. As Gangubai herself solemnly stated, "I could not afford it. If I sent Krishna for a concert, they would pay her half of what they paid me. As it is, with what I earned, it was hard to run the show. How could we have managed with lesser?" But it wasn't so simple, though this may have been a genuine reason.

The biggest jolt in Gangubai's life was the death of her mother. She was so attached to Ambabai that her unanticipated death created an emotional vacuum that nobody could ever fill. Krishna was similar to Ambabai. She had the same health issues. Krishna was inseparable from Gangubai from her childhood. It had resulted in a strong, possessive bond. She feared that allowing Krishna to become an independent concert musician would take her away. Krishna would then begin to have a life of her own, a world of her own, make her own decisions—the possibility of physically moving away from her loomed large. Gangubai could never come to terms with such a change.

Hence, she never discussed it. Even when very dear friends like Susheela and Vijaya Mulay asked Gangubai why she was not getting Krishna married, her answer was hardly convincing. She would often skirt the question with some inane answer. "She's not too well, you see …"

Perhaps when Krishna was in her prime, she didn't take marriage too seriously. The difficulties of her mother's life could have acted as a deterrent. Moreover, her passionate attachment to her music made her feel that marriage and children would come in the way of her life as a full-fledged and busy musician, which was how she imagined herself in the future. Krishna knew her potential as a concert musician, and hoped that someday in the future she would be one. Little did she know that life had different plans for her. If Gangubai was a Mogubai, she would have stopped singing to make way for her daughter, like Mogubai did for Kishori Amonkar. And if that had happened, Krishna's name would be taken with other women musicians of her generation like Prabha Atre, Parveen Sultana and Malini Rajurkar.

"We had too many financial constraints. My mother could not afford to stop singing to make way for my sister," Babanna used to say. In the later years of her life, Krishna did want to get married. If not a career in music, she wanted at least a family of her own. She was sad with the way her life was shaping up, but not once did she utter a word. "If only I had a son, I would surely get him married to your daughter," she would tell her niece Vaishnavi, as she helped the young mother and her newborn.

Krishna did cut a few albums, gave a few performances, but she was not allowed to have a blazing career. She won the Rajyotsava Award, became an A-grade artiste at All India Radio, but couldn't go further.

Gangubai lived a life of denial and suppression. Krishna partook of this suppression. In later years, when Gangubai had crossed eighty, she slowly began to make way for Krishna. By then Krishna had been diagnosed with cancer, and had even undergone a surgery. She had recovered well, and went back to accompanying her mother on concert tours. During this period, Krishna gave a few independent concerts as well. She earned a good name and was being hailed as the true successor of Gangubai's music. In December 2002, Krishna was invited for the Gwalior Tansen Samaroh. She was extremely happy about this invitation and had gone out of her way to make preparations for the concert, despite her wavering health. Gangubai was ninety, but insisted on accompanying Krishna. Babanna and Dr Tavarageri went along with the mother and daughter. Gangubai was overjoyed with the overwhelming response Krishna received in Gwalior. She may have been trying to correct her wrongs, but it was rather late in the day.

From there they proceeded to Bombay, where Gangubai had a performance. After the concert, at the Bombay station Gangubai felt dizzy. Thank God for Babanna and the doctor who accompanied them, Gangubai was safely brought to Hubli and was immediately rushed to the hospital. Tests revealed that she had bone cancer. For the family members it was as if they had been struck by a bolt from hell. The treatment had to start immediately. Krishna stood like a rock by her mother, and was at her beck and call. If she could serve her mother despite her own health condition, one can only attribute it to her enormous love and indomitable will.

From Krishna's friends one finds that even at this juncture in her life, she had not lost hopes of making it as an independent concert artiste. The Gwalior response had triggered fresh hopes and new dreams in her. But fate had its own plans. Krishna's illness resurfaced, and despite intensive treatment, she did not survive. In 2004, she passed away. The true carrier of Gangubai's music—in letter and spirit—was no more. Gangubai had lost her dear daughter and a dearer companion. Krishna had permanently moved into the dark shadows.

Late years

I knew that giving an account of Gangubai's life was a formidable enterprise. Entering her interiority, experiencing her truths, and then turning these abstractions into my own language, was daunting. I was full of doubts and uncertainties, and with each meeting I realized I knew less and less of her.

Her life was full of suffering, but it was never dull with joyless pessimism. She always had an unseen reserve of energy to bounce back from any no-exit situation. Not that Gangubai was hallowed by some cosmic revelation, she was far too grounded. Her deep faith in the essence of things that could exist independently of their physical manifestations was hard to understand. She took the name of her god, Mylaralinga, every now and then. The Buddha's Middle Path was concerned with how to live vitally, spiritedly and intelligently in a dysfunctional world—this is the path Gangubai walked. Her disposition often reminded me of the Buddha, "Suffering alone exists, but none who suffer."

* * *

Gangubai had been fortunate as well. She had benefited from the English enterprise of the gramophone and the radio. She was also the beneficiary of royal patronage. She was lucky to meet the great masters, who with their highly democratic vision bowed to these phenomenally talented women and even carried them through rough social periods. Of course, Gangubai and her unyielding conviction stood the test of time. "I travelled the entire length and breadth of this country," she would say, recalling her friend N.K.'s comment in an interview, who said: "Like the Ganga in your name, you flow from the Himalayas. But your daughter, like the river Krishna, is the pride of the state."

Gangubai received all the prestigious awards of the state and the country. She received doctorates and several titles as well. Her seventy-fifth birthday in 1988 was a very big affair celebrated at the Sawai Gandharva Hall, Hubli. Under the leadership of Dr S.S. Gore, the Academy of Performing Arts organized the felicitation ceremony. A stunning bilingual felicitation volume was brought out on the occasion: novelist Dr S.L. Bhyrappa and musicologist Sadananda Kanavalli edited the Kannada volume, and Dr Ashok Ranade edited the English one. The stage was star-studded, the huge guest list comprised Shivaram Karanth, H.Y. Sharada Prasad, Bhimsen Joshi, Firoze Dastur, Jasraj and the three editors of the felicitation volume. The hall was packed, and people had to wait outside. To coincide with this, Vijaya Mulay had made a film on Gangubai, in which she had famously said: "If a man becomes a musician they call him Ustad and Pandit, but a woman continues to remain a Bai—like Kesarbai, Mogubai and Gangubai." That evening, after the felicitation, Gangubai performed what would be an oft-remembered rendition of *Marwa*.

Following this, the Gandharva Mahavidyalaya organized a felicitation for Gangubai and the chief guest was the late President, R. Venkataraman. Speaking at the felicitation at the IIT convocation hall in Delhi, the principal of the school, Vinay Mudgal, had said, "The world should never forget that Gangubai never used her art as a tool to make money. She learnt from one of the finest disciples of Abdul Karim Khan saab, Sawai Gandharva, and never swayed away from the path on which her guru led her. She rendered her guru's teachings with the utmost sincerity."

Gangubai went on to receive the Deenanath Mangeshkar Award, the Ganayogi Panchakshara Award and the Kanaka Purandara Award. When she turned eighty-five in 1998, the Ninad Music Company organized a huge felicitation ceremony in

Bombay's Nehru Centre. On this occasion Delhi University not only conferred a doctorate on her, but also honoured her with the Manik Ratna Award.

Apart from her domestic role, Gangubai had just one other identity: of a musician. Though she had several hidden layers to her personality, they never had a chance to manifest themselves. Grinding domesticity and an equally daunting musical world filled her life. However, in 1993-94, Gangubai was nominated as a member of the legislative council. When she was forced to make speeches in all kinds of fora—at police department functions, schools and offices—one could glimpse her political positions. "Even my music performances began to have speeches. I was never a speaker, but since I had taken on this office, people expected me to talk. I am a great lover of literature, I have read voraciously all my life, but that never taught me how to speak!" she would grin. It was true, Gangubai was not much of a speaker, but whatever little she said made great sense. If she was invited again and again as chief guest by so many, it was not only because she was a legendary musician who also held an important office, but because of her ability to state lofty things as if they were native truths. It wouldn't be far-fetched to say that the legendary musician became a public persona with this phase. It was beyond her to grapple with falsities, and she never said anything merely for effect.

When the ABC Corporation brought the Miss Universe contest to Bangalore, Gangubai was among the early protestors. She stood up spontaneously to say her bit: "In Chandragutti, women offer nude worship to the gods out of their devotion and faith. Nevertheless, it is a superstition and we cannot condone it. The government is perhaps right in banning it, because the thousands of onlookers who gather there don't share the faith of the worshippers. Isn't the Miss Universe contest, where women flaunt their bodies for the wrong reasons, worse than Chandragutti? It is not even an act of faith. Shouldn't the government ban it?" Others in the group were struck by the manner in which Gangubai articulated her thoughts, and congratulated her for it. But for Gangubai it was all too real. She knew the shackles that allow the body to take precedence over the soul. Stigma attached to this was hard to forget.

When she became the chairman of the annual music conference of Gayana Samaja in 1985, Gangubai said something that was equally sincere and heartfelt. "The learned say that music is the path to reach God. All our ancient Bhakti saints and composers have said this—everyone from Swami Haridas to Tyagaraja. For me, music is not the path to God but God itself. To realize this God, I had to achieve a deep understanding of my music. This was my constant longing. My salvation came from satisfying my guru and my listeners. Music is not something that you achieve by intelligence and skill. It is not even something that you achieve by mastering the theories. You stand a chance only when you can become a slave of your guru, and labour at his feet day and night. Without a guru, nothing is ever possible. My guru lives within me as my life force." Ram Shri Mugali, a big name in the Kannada literary world, was among the chief guests that evening. He walked up to Gangubai and congratulated her for what she said. Gangubai moved people with the power of truth and her simplicity of thought.

Gangubai would say in her later years how she never aspired to achieve more than her inheritance allowed her. From the beginning, it was her aim to perfect what was passed on to her and render it with devotion. "In this process, there have been moments when I have experienced intense emotion, moments of godliness … I consulted Agnihotri Shankar Bhatt on my experience, and he told me that these were brief experiences of awakening of consciousness and that I should try to hold on to them for longer periods. Maybe it was true, for Khan saab too had spoken of a heightened spiritual experience through *sur sadhana*." She would utter these words with no superior air of a sadhaka, but in total perplexity before the mystery of music.

It was true that she believed in strictly adhering to the *gharana* tradition. It was a personal belief and never a dogma. Her own *gurubandhu* Bhimsen Joshi drank from all streams of music and found a musical personality that was distinctly his own, and Gangubai had great regard for his monstrous talent. But she would never tolerate her own students swaying away from the Sawai Gandharva style.

In the last stages of her life her memory may have deteriorated, but she knew of the new trends in the world of music—how Lakshmikant Pyarelal had changed the Hindi music scene with *Hum Aapke Hain Kaun.* She was aware that fusion music was of interest to many, even as she advised against blending the two grand traditions. She continued to hold forth on many things, and never in an ill-informed way.

"Why do we have so many academies, *sabha*s and organizations? It is their primary duty to preserve classical music," she would say. "There are several schools that now propagate music, for instance the Gandharva Mahavidyalaya. In such schools it is impossible to teach music of any one *gharana.* There will be a synthesis of many styles and thoughts, and meaningful processes emerge from these places as well. Maybe in the coming years, the characteristic features of different *gharana*s will fade and what will remain is a collective (*samanvaya*) kind of music. In terms of unifying people, maybe it will be good, who knows ..." she would muse.

There are some things for which you never find answers: Gangubai, who was such a strong votary of the *guru-shishya parampara*, a musician who believed that the guru was the light of one's life, could never actually train students like her guru, Sawai Gandharva, did. In fact, this is true of all her contemporaries as well—Mansur, Kumar Gandharva and Bhimsen Joshi. Except Basavaraj Rajguru, none of these musicians dedicated time to shape and mould musical talents. All of them did have students, who were but hardly a match to the monumental figures their teachers were. These musicians were not as lucky as Abdul Karim Khan or Sawai Gandharva, who had students outshining them as well as furthering the music of the *gharana.* In Gangubai's case, the answers to why this could have happened are more or less obvious. And maybe one should find comfort in the obvious.

Everyone had access to Gangubai, she had no trace of dogmatism in her and was very willing to listen to one and all. People longed to meet her and, when they did, she made it seem like she was longing to meet them. If you didn't know her from close quarters, it was easy to misconstrue her politics, in fact, many such analyses have emerged after a one-off meeting with her.

The BJP was trying to build its base in North Karnataka, and Manoj was a party worker and a lawyer. As a result several people of different ideological affiliations visited their Hubli home. From the staunch Uma Bharati, to the writer and admirer of Gangubai's music S.L. Bhyrappa, who has been an upholder of right-wing politics, a range of people visited her. Soon, there would be articles about her alleged "RSS interests". On many an occasion, this has been a topic of discussion with Manoj, at one time Uma Bharti's advocate, who was also in a way responsible for this tag. He would say, "*Ajji*, beyond all this. She welcomed everyone as a perfect host. But propagating Hindu ideology in the RSS way was not her thing." Manoj, who has inherited his *ajji*'s transparency, used to admit to the foolhardiness of his days as a party worker, and said, "Somewhere along the way, I realized that this wasn't who I am… I am completely dedicated to organizing music. That's the mission of my life, and the only way I can be one with my grandmother's spirit …"

* * *

Once the reports of scans and tests were out, the doctors simply refused to allow her to travel.

Apart from frequent bouts of giddiness, Gangubai suffered from severe back pain. Gradually, she found it difficult to walk and climb stairs. To make things worse, her kidneys were in no great condition either. A series of tests and examinations followed. An abnormal mass of tissue that was detected was sent for a biopsy. The results were not favourable at all. Babanna was summoned, and her condition was explained to him. Her reports were then sent to the Tata Cancer Hospital in Bombay.

Gangubai was so dear to the people of Hubli–Dharwad that a host of doctors offered themselves in service to her. Eventually, a team of ten best doctors was chosen.

Gangubai's case was handed over to Dr Anita Borges of Tata Cancer Hospital in Bombay, who was an expert on such cases. She concluded that Gangubai's condition was Non-Hodgkin's Lymphoma, and it had spread to her entire back region. Dr Smriti Krishna from the Tata Cancer Institute came down to Hubli with the reports and, out of great respect and admiration for the legendary singer, took charge of Gangubai's treatment. The cancer expert, along with a team of ten committed doctors from Hubli, started the treatment on a war footing. After several rounds of discussion she personally administered Mabthera, the monoclonal antibodies and radiotherapy. She also guided the initial chemotherapy sessions as Gangubai was well past ninety and in a fairly delicate condition. Dr Smriti laid out the plan of the entire treatment and left a detailed schedule with Dr Kalamdani before she left Hubli.

"After Krishna was diagnosed with cancer in 2001, I saw her go through chemotherapy and a couple of surgeries … The poor girl braved the pain with such equanimity. All my life I have been mortally scared of hospitals and doctors, but when this happened, I made up my mind to go through it bravely. Krishna had set an example … Of course, age was not on my side, and neither did my body have that kind of strength, but I resolved to go through with it."

The chemotherapy shots were phenomenally expensive. During the initial phase, she had to undergo several rounds of treatment. Like any other cancer patient, Gangubai too experienced the trauma and the after-effects of the treatment. But she braved everything so positively that she could recover despite being on the other side of ninety. In fact, a couple of years before she died, Manoj brought out a booklet called *Cancer? Hedarabedi* (Cancer? Do Not Fear) with *ajji*'s consent, where she narrated her medical experience alongside photographs recording her in the various stages of her treatment. This, along with a red rose, was distributed to every single patient in the Cancer Hospital.

Krishna, who had recovered by then, was at the service of her mother. She was so patient and loving that it was impossible not to feel good in her care. But the most worrying aspect of it all was the expenses. "I was in no state to afford this expensive disease. We spent many anxious days wondering what to do. We had already spent a lot for Krishna's treatment ..." The Karnataka government's decision to provide her medical aid came as a godsend. Gangubai would recall with gratitude their decision to help her, and also that of the Hubli–Dharwad Muncipal Corporation.

After intensive treatment, in about six months, Gangubai had recovered and was able to walk. The doctors said, her positive outlook made her recovery possible. Dr S.A. Miraj, who was on the team of doctors, had said, "When she was told that she had cancer, she took it so well. I have seen patients weeping bitterly. But she found out what her mode of treatment was, and went through it without complaining. I used to ask her what gave her the strength and she would say, 'I am not scared of death.'"

Talking about her ailment Gangubai would say, "There isn't much you can do to escape fate. For me, lying in bed incapacitated was unthinkable. I was always thinking of my music, interacting with my students and accompanists ... I wanted to be done with the treatment as soon as possible and get back to my music." Her family and the doctors of Hubli left no stone unturned in mobilizing the best for Gangubai. Towards the end of 2003, she felt better. However, this didn't last because Krishna's illness worsened in early 2004. By September that year, Krishna was no more. Her pain, suffering and eventual death left Gangubai terribly shaken. Her daughter, who was her companion and friend, and who had spent over seventy years with her, never to be separated from her even for a day, was gone.

Gangubai, once again, went into her shell. She became extremely withdrawn, and hardly spoke to anyone. She cut off her connections with music, refusing to listen to it, sing, teach her students, or even talk about music. Gangubai wept often for Krishna.

The family was unsettled by her grief—they had their own grief to bear. They were coping with Krishna's death in their own way. Krishna, who had been the lifeline of the family, had tended to each person's need with zest and devotion. With her gone, they had certainly been derailed, but Gangubai's reaction to Krishna's death threatened to destabilize them.

While most of the grandchildren were prepared to accept their grandmother in her present state, Manoj was not ready to do so. He had built his universe around his grandmother, and if she suffered silently, it would surely affect them. He took on the task of gradually bringing her back to normal. He spent hours talking to her—telling her the many stories of her life, the difficulties she encountered, the hardship of her *riyaz*, and how she offered herself to music. Was there any meaning to Gangubai's life dissociated from music?—he asked her every single day. The past had not been forgotten, but the death of her daughter was so overwhelming that it had gone into hiding. Slowly, when Manoj cleared the cobwebs of distress, Gangubai realized the truth of what Manoj was saying: what was her life without music? If she did not throw herself back into her music, there was no way she could survive the remaining years: wasn't that the way in which she coped with the deaths of her mother, her guru and Ramanna?

She was experiencing intense inner turmoil. Slowly and quietly, she came out of those moments of anguish, her spindly fingers holding on to Manoj's sturdy ones. Until her death, which came five years later, Manoj took on the role of Krishna: he was not a musician, and could not provide her *saath.* But he was always there for his *ajji.* Gangubai and Manoj got into several arguments. She chided him, and in return Manoj also reprimanded her—but she knew he cared. In her last moments at the hospital, Gangubai held on to Manoj's hands lovingly. Manoj had his own way of dealing with her, making fun of her, teasing her, shouting at her, pushing her to do things she didn't want to, forcing her to go out and attend programmes … He told her, in these ways, that she was very important to their lives, and Gangubai understood him in all his coarseness. There were occasions when she was bitterly angry with him, but she would snap out of her anger soon. Of course, apart from Manoj, her dear sons Babanna and Narayan, and Lalithakka who never crossed the threshold of the kitchen and her room, stood firmly with her—nurturing and protecting her like a little baby.

As she got on with her life, she became so busy that every second day she had a function to attend. Gangubai loved being with people. The warmth of her community brought her cheer. There were days when her body refused to cope with her spirit, and she would become grumpy. I can never forget the way she fussed over the sari she had to wear to Kundagol in September 2007 for Sawai Gandharva's *Punyathithi.* She had consulted everyone who walked into the room, and was unhappy because no one made the right choice: no one suggested the soft, light pink silk sari that she was determined to wear. This went on for hours, and finally Manoj hollered from the drawing room, "What's wrong with you? You don't have to come, stay here worrying about silly things …" She retorted angrily, and her feeble voice crossed the room. "What do you mean, don't come? You stay put, I will summon a car and go. It's my guru's *Punyathithi, hanh* ..." she snapped angrily. Manoj always knew how to achieve the desired results with her. That day, she was the first one to leave, starting much before the rest of us set out. And by the time we reached, she had inspected the dining hall on her wheelchair and was calling out to all those who walked past her, checking what bit of organizing was allotted to them, and whether they had done their job or not.

The way Gangubai came back from her illness and how she coped with the shock of Krishna's death was rather remarkable. Her student of many years, Ashok Nadiger, organized his *Ganda Bandhan* ceremony in Kundagol in 2005. After the formal ceremony was over, Gangubai insisted on singing and gave tense moments to everyone. She would not stop and went on for a good forty-five minutes! "I regained my lost connection with the world of music. I felt I could sing again," she confessed later. Gangubai had returned to singing after a long hiatus of nearly two years, and this gave her a big reason to live on.

Having regained her confidence, Gangubai plunged back into public life with the enthusiasm of a twenty-year-old. When S.M. Krishna was the governor of Maharashtra, he felicitated her. Gangubai had such strong ties with Bombay that she couldn't refuse to go. She wanted to show Maharashtrians, her ardent patrons, that she was still around and in perfect mental health. With amazing grit, she got on to her wheelchair and decided to go. "I pushed away the wheelchair once I stepped on stage, and walked fifteen steps without anyone's help," she was grinning. "I had to show them that I was not an old woman!"

She resumed teaching. The few students she had, who were deeply attached to her, were only too happy to have her back. Gangubai made several difficult trips in her last few years. Within Hubli and Dharwad she was the chief guest at over three hundred programmes. She travelled all the way to Goa by car for another felicitation. She went to Pune to inaugurate the Marathi and Kannada Theatre Festival. Having gone to Pune, she couldn't miss seeing her dear Bhimu. She sat down with him and shared notes on their old age: both were ailing, but she had the fortitude to struggle, while Bhimu was confined to his wheelchair and bed. Sangli, Gulbarga, Gadag—Gangubai went wherever she was invited. Her warmth and cheer was infectious. Everyone loved her and looked after her as if she were their own grandmother. Gangubai, too, allowed everyone to take care of her.

When she went to Kolhapur for a programme in 2008, a year before her death, the organizers learnt of her desire to visit the Mahalakshmi Temple and took her there. The priests took her straight into the sanctum sanctorum, much to her embarrassment, and gave her the privilege of seeing the deity from up close. "Maybe it was their love and affection that made it possible for me to sing for the goddess," Gangubai never lost a chance to count her blessings. Having gone to Kolhapur she insisted on being taken to Miraj. She went to Abdul Karim Khan saab's tomb and paid her respects. Those were indeed her last respects.

In the hectic last years of her life, Manoj stood by Gangubai unflinchingly, took her where she desired to go, and kept her in constant touch with people. She was all too fragile, and such frequent travel was rather risky. There was a lot of criticism about this in the Hubli–Dharwad music circles as well. "She is too precious to waste her life locked up in a room brooding about her illness," Manoj would say. Gangubai infused warmth everywhere she went. In return, she also received a great amount of affection.

* * *

Even as Gangubai travelled like there was no tomorrow in the last few years of her life, she visited the hospital just as frequently. After a lively day of outing and felicitation, Gangubai's little room would be packed with friends and visitors. Gangubai would always have a story for everyone, and in the background she would keep grumbling about her health. If their domestic help had left for the day, Babanna and Lalithakka made sure that the tea kept coming.

Even when she was lying in the hospital bed, Gangubai was so full of life. The doctors and nurses loved her. It was difficult to get her to stop talking in her last years. Potamma, her personal nurse, who spent all her time with Gangubai in the last ten years, was very indulgent towards her. Even when *ajji* was in a foul mood, Potamma's voice would never change from her gentle, soft tones; the smile from her face never faded. She could not bear to see *ajji* in pain, she absorbed every tantrum with unbelievable patience, and there was no doubt about *ajji*'s fondness for her. "What time is Potamma coming?" "Potamma will do that for me …"—Potamma this, Potamma that, Potamma was always on her breath. When *ajji* died, Potamma was inconsolable. She sat next to the body in the Hubli Glass House, and at home till *ajji* was cremated. "It must have been *punya* that I earned from my last birth that I got to serve someone like her …" Potamma had wept.

Each time Gangubai was admitted to the hospital in 2009, I would rush to Hubli. It had more or less become a routine—once every two to three weeks. The last time I visited her was in the end of June 2009. She looked very frail and tired. Her speech had become very incoherent. She had not lost her memory, even though it was all one big jumble. Her mind would course through an event, jump to another and yet another, before ending at a completely different point. Her enthusiasm was not consistent. But her warmth and affection had not dimmed even a bit. I stayed with her for five days, and reminiscences from that conversation follow.

* * *

"Come," she gestured with her frail fingers through the glass window of the ICU chamber. *Raatri gaadige bandyenu* (Did you come by the night train)? she asked me, holding my hand weakly. With frequent shivers and bouts of fever she looked very tired. "I hope you went home and ate something? Were Babu and Lalitha there?" she asked, feeling drowsy with the sedatives that were being pumped into her body.

There was hardly an occasion when her simplicity did not leave me overwhelmed. Even if you looked hard, you wouldn't find in her a trace of the queen of the Kirana *gharana* that she was. In her puny form, this outstanding musician with her once thundering voice had sunk into the folds and creases of the hospital bed and looked a tired, little sparrow. "The only good thing about coming to a hospital is that lots of people visit you," she would say with her childlike grin, "and you know how much I love people, *nanaga mandi bhaala sertaara*," she would add. "But I want to go home …"

"I always go to Kalamdani Hospital. This time they have brought me to this different place … what's it called?" she asked the nurse who had just stepped into her cubicle. "Maybe they had to treat a person more important than me at Kalamdani's, that's why they have sent me to this hospital …" she would come up with her own naive reasons.

"Do you know Bendre?" she asked a junior doctor who had some time on hand and had stepped in for a chat. "He taught me for a while at the National School. You know, we had a music teacher who would say '*sammkula*' for '*sankula*' …" she had recalled with a giggle the ninety-year-old episode. By this time, other doctors and nurses had also gathered around Gangubai, joining in the laughter. "Tell us more, tell us more …" they pleaded, and *ajji* was only waiting for such a request. She regaled them with incidents about how people who listened to her on the radio thought she was a man and how her plain, village bumpkin looks put her in difficult situations. Gangubai loved making fun of herself. And as she laughed, she got breathless and incoherent, but who could stop her?

The nurse sensed that if she allowed *ajji* to speak further, it could get dangerous. She got tough with all the visitors and sent everyone away. "I am going home early tomorrow morning, so may not see you …" she told them with certainity, as if she had just returned from a meeting with the doctors. "Come home after ten days and I will teach you the song we sang at the Belgaum Congress when Gandhiji came. I will be fine by then …"

Those ten days, people kept streaming into her ward in the hospital. Most of them did not know her personally. Hundreds waited in front of the hospital, hoping they would be allowed in. The minute they saw Manoj or Babanna's face they would run up to them and ask, "*Akkaru hegiddarree* (How is *akka*)?" A boy in his seventh standard turned up on two consecutive days with flowers and waited till it was dark. He was finally allowed to see *ajji*. *Ningondu uppa kodla* (Shall I give you a kiss)? and then, *ajji* had kissed him on his palm. "Study well, it's a great joy for your parents …" she said, holding his hand lovingly.

"Give me my comb, and put a little powder on my face," she would tell her nurse, "apparently, some minister is coming to see me …" She insisted that her hospital gown had to be covered with a shawl. "I can't look old and dirty," she would say angrily with childlike innocence.

Gangubai was meticulous and disciplined about whatever she did: be it her music or everyday household duties. "These hospital visits have left me with no time to clean the rice … ummm …"

she would mutter to herself, and turning to me soon after that, "It's seven o'clock. Go home before it gets dark. I will be there early tomorrow morning. Be there, don't go away. Let's have tea together," she had said, every evening of my five-day stay.

* * *

I met Gangubai well after the peak of her musical career. Like the millions of this country, I too had been stirred by her unadorned, austere music. I had stepped into her home, Ganga Lahari, with enormous regard for the great musician. Knowing her as a person only heightened my reverence for her. There was no dichotomy between Gangubai the musician and the individual.

After this hospital stay, she had returned home, only to go back within two days. And this time she could not come home. Every day, Manoj gave me an update without getting irritated by my frequent calls. On the night of 20 July, at around 11 p.m., Manoj had said, "*Ajji* is very unstable. She is losing her will. The doctors aren't giving us too much hope …" He then reassuringly said: "Wait till tomorrow. I will tell you if you need to come." The next morning, at 7.05 a.m., Manoj's call came and, with his usual quickness that barely revealed any of his emotions, he said, "*Ajji hodlu. Horatu baa* (Ajji's gone. Come)."

In about half an hour, I was on the road to Hubli. It was the most painful journey—my memories of her coalesced with her own and left an unbearable mass in my throat.

When I reached Hubli late that afternoon, it was drizzling. Her body had been kept in the glass house and there was a long queue of people waiting to pay their last respects to her. A huge number of *bhajana mandali*s had gathered under the *pandal*, and were singing for Gangubai, one after the other, endlessly. In every corner of the huge field, unmindful of the rain, groups of people huddled together discussing how a great era had come to pass. Some were crying inconsolably, as if they had lost a close member of their family. The whole place was fragrant with the scent of *agarbatti*s. Potamma was sitting beside *ajji*'s body. Grandchildren and great-grandchildren arrived. Ministers, bureaucrats came. None could believe that she was gone. Everyone had a personal story to tell: what she had told them when they met her. Late in the evening, *ajji*'s body was brought to Ganga Lahari. Before the body arrived, hundreds gathered near the house. Someone had put up a *pandal* in the compound and singing groups had already assembled. Babanna, Lalithakka and the rest of the family suddenly felt completely out of control in the situation, and fixed themselves in front of the television. They were moving between channels, obsessing about who is saying what about Gangubai, how much footage they have: "Oh, that was in 1990!", "That was at Shakti Sthal"—saying so, Babanna interrupted the family gathering every now and then. A strange emptiness was filling into all of them. The centre point of their lives was no more: what would they now fill it up with? "Babanna, apparently the State will do the honours … This was just announced," one of the grandsons said. "*Yaava channelnaago* (On which channel was it announced)?" Baba asked and was once again flipping through channels.

All that spirits desire, spirits attain

The next day, 22 July 2009, obituaries flooded the newspapers. In *The Guardian*, *The Independent*, *Los Angeles Times*, various national and regional newspapers and a whole lot of magazines and journals, everyone paid their tribute to the doyenne. Almost all of them recognized that a glorious period in the cultural history of the nation had come to a close. In the life and music of Gangubai, it was not merely the singular presence of Hubli–Dharwad and the extraordinary Kirana lineage that had lost its burning lamp. The manifold cultural histories of music and theatre, which came together from various, far-flung geographical locations and seemingly unknown contexts, had also lost an emblem. In Gangubai were melded the stories of women of outstanding courage and conviction, the stories of an era that upheld values of a tradition over the individual self. Astonishingly, many social-historical moments and junctures, several sturdy artistic spirits, the journey of the nation: all these narratives had collapsed into her own personal history. In the death of Gangubai, these movements of the past had come to an end, after having reached an apogee.

Most articles invariably narrated the story of her life: her struggles and hardships, her humiliations, and her indomitable spirit that rose above the cruelties of caste and gender. They recalled her contemporaries, spoke to her kith and kin in Dharwad, recirculated those numerous anecdotes warmly, most of which were already in the public realm. Curiously, hardly any of the obituaries spoke about her music, and even if they did they were broad brushstrokes like "the androgynous power of her voice" or "the thunder in her masculine voice". In fact, one of them was presumptuous enough to assert that Gangubai was not competent enough to discuss her music, because she always regaled interviewers with stories and said nothing about her music! When musicians of national standing wrote their tributes, like Kishori Amonkar and Ustad Amjad Ali Khan, they too said little about her music, but had a lot to say about what a fine human being she was. This was true of Rajeev Taranath and Shubha Mudgal as well. It was perhaps impossible to separate her persona from her music. However, one newspaper editoral made an important observation: "She did not stray away from the *khayal* style which she had mastered at the feet of her teacher. What made her among the greatest exponents of the Kirana *gharana* was not just her natural gifts, training and expertise but also her sincerity and the feeling for elemental sound."

Gangubai had relocated her music to a new space, keeping her inherited musical values intact. Why did everyone speak of her leonine voice and not about her complex imagination that expressed itself in a very simple narrative? Had Gangubai's music—so shorn of embellishment and frills—stopped fascinating this generation fed on gimmickry and standardization? Did everything begin and end with voice, for which she herself attached little value? She never dared to experiment: there were very few dramatic moments in her music that resulted from a show of technical mastery, but she dazzled her audience with her aesthetic brilliance, with a rhetoric that was deeply emotional. Her musical insights and their articulation marked a bygone historical moment that was profoundly spiritual and devotional, and emerged from her total surrender to a great tradition and its masters. Times had changed, and music had changed too. But Gangubai had guarded her creative space with exacting austerity. She was arrogant about it as well. If we were not talking about it, did it mean that we no longer had the language for it? Was it no longer a part of what formed our musical imagination?

D.K. Pattamal, six years younger than Gangubai, died five days before she did. Both these remarkable women born in pre-Independence India, one a victim of orthodoxy and the other of ostracization, were pioneers in their respective fields. Both were beneficiaries of the technological advancements during the turn of the century, and, in their music, one glimpsed their shared understanding of the nature of art and of the artistic climate of the times they represented.

In a tribute to both these artistes, musician T.V. Gopalakrishnan wrote in *The Indian Express*: "Both were the purist's delight. If Gangubai was a flag-bearer of the Kirana *gharana* style of North Indian music, Pattamal was equally reputed for her allegiance to the weighty rendition of the Carnatic idiom. There was never an iota of gimmickry, and both had a base voice. They upheld the core aesthetics of their traditions."

Gangubai, like Pattamal, he said, focused on the dense areas of her music system. Expansive, bold-sounding *khayal*s consumed the chunk of her performances. This was typically like Pattamal, who was known for her grand delineation of the structurally intricate Dikshitar *kriti*s and complex *ragam-tanam-pallavi*s. Both believed in the merits of the *gurukula* system and stuck to it till their last breath.

M.L. Vasanthakumari (MLV), who came from socially difficult circumstances, was relatively modern in her outlook compared to these two musicians. She was a master of technique and easily took on intellectual challenges, much like her revolutionary guru G.N. Balasubramaniam. Her artistic expression was therefore clearly different, but she was also someone who rested total faith in tradition. She strongly disapproved of those who wanted to outshine their teachers, and unabashedly termed it *adhikaprasangam*! MLV was clear that a good *shishya* evolved a style of her own, it formed a part of her articulated set of beliefs, whereas in Pattamal and Gangubai it remained a part of their "unsaid".

Hirabai Badodekar, who was instrumental in bestowing dignity upon female musicianship, had a striking silken voice and her music was imbued with nobility. Prabha Atre, in a monograph on this powerful representative of the Kirana *gharana*, wrote that she was faithful to the style of the *gharana* despite a stunning musical mind that was all her own. There was no aggressiveness or pretence. Her music was infused with the same humility, politeness and absorption as her own personality.

Most of these women, who were exceptional artists, lived their lives and their music with a commitment that was so rare. Despite their hardships, they were uncompromising practitioners of their art and exhibited an intense emotional attachment to their music. Their music was *bhava*-laden and impassioned. Kesarbai Kerkar, a consummate artiste who was extremely severe with people, continues to be remembered for her monumental singing. When it came to music and her gurus, she melted into devotion. When she went to seek her guru Alladiya Khan saab's guidance, he had forbidden her from stage performances even though she was an established artiste. During the next twenty-five years, not once did Kesarbai speak of her desire to perform. Alladiya Khan was a believer in unconditional *sadhana*, and Kesarbai worshipped every word he said. She took great pride in being the authentic exponent and custodian of her guru's *gayaki*, but the art itself was something ethereal, beyond the bounds of the human world. This musician of august virtuosity would say: "For seven decades I have sung for the gods. If incidentally, I have pleased listeners, I am doubly fulfilled."

The opening lines of M.S. Subbulakshmi's presidential address at the Music Academy in 1968 were most poignant. The diva of Carnatic music, who was trained by the most illustrious gurus—Semmangudi Srinivasa Iyer, Ariyakudi Ramanuja Iyengar, T. Brinda, Nedunuri Krishnamurthy from whom she learnt Sanskrit, Pt. Narayanrao Vyas—chose to pay obeisance to her mother Shamughavadivu, a veena player par excellence, over all her gurus. In doing so, Subbulakshmi had not only placed before the world the remarkable musicianship of Shanmughavadivu that shaped and refined her sensibilities, but also put on record her transition from Shanmughavadivu's circumstances. "At a time like this when a woman is called upon to preside over this conference, it is but natural that the memory of her mother should come before her mind's eye," she said. "In my case, my mother was not merely my mother, she was also my music teacher. What little knowledge of music I possess today, I owe it, in the first instance, to my mother, the late Veena Shanmukhavadivu of Madurai. Before her, both as mother and music teacher, I prostrate and pray for her soul force to come to my aid." Shanmughavadivu's reputation, like that of Ambabai, Gangubai's mother, brought the best of musicians to her doorstep, with whom she would have enlightened discussions. But she was not fortunate, and remained far from centre stage. When MS was conferred the Sangita Kalanidhi, the first for a woman musician, she remembered Veena Dhanammal, the great musician from her childhood. "She rested great faith in my music and had foreseen a bright future for me," she had said.

Most of these women musicians of the late nineteenth and early twentieth centuries lived in pain and penury. However, the urge of their intellectual consciousness soared above all the hurdles and shackles of the material world. They were like any other human being given to highs and lows, ups and downs, desires and temptations, but as far as their art was concerned they remained fearlessly truthful and tremendously self-demanding. No material temptations could take them one step away from their fervour. The story of Siddheshwari Devi's childhood haunts you for its abject misery. But despite a miserable life she, out of her own seeking, became the queen of *thumri.* Her unique classicism captured an emotional and artistic spontaneity.

Veena Dhanammal, who lived, breathed and dreamt music all her life, was infinitely refined about her music and the style it embodied. She passed away around the same time as Ambabai, in the 1930s. Her music was not an aggressive display of technique, but a highly introspective identification with the intangible elements of melody and song. It shunned gimmicks and freely embraced classicism. For her, nothing else was more important in her music than the crux of the idea. Dhanammal did not achieve the recognition she deserved in her lifetime, but it did not matter to her.

Most of these women, whose journeys were roughly coeval with Gangubai's own time, were victims of social discrimination. Rasoolan Bai, Jaddan Bai, Anjanibai Malpekar, Gauhar Jan, Zohrabai Agrewali, and a whole lot of others who vanished into the creases of the past were on par, at times even better, than the legendary masters of music. Almost all of them were able to bring into their music that most elusive thing: devotion. Their understanding of their music was so complete that their complex intellectual ideas often translated into lasting and moving emotional experiences. They constructed and rendered their music with a virtuosity that penetrated consciousness. Through the movements they conducted in their music, they quietly altered the course of cultural history for posterity. T. Brinda had entered the domain of male aesthetics, she had even unearthed all of Kshetrayya's compositions. Lalithangi (MLV's mother) had dusted the cobwebs on Purandaradasa's writings and M.S. Annamacharya's lyrics. The three had revived the pre-Trinity *vaggeyakara*s. When social opprobrium on women in the public sphere was at its peak, these women were the silent architects of a century.

Why do I, when I have told the story of Gangubai, remember all these women? Do I fear that her era has vanished, and that all those glorious moments and living memories will only survive as chronicles? Gangubai lived in a specific place and time. Was her context just her own? Why was my canvas filling up with memories, stories and heroic acts of all these women who occupied different historical locations? There was a certain truth that was emerging out of Gangubai's life, but that truth was not given: it could not be fixed. It was expanding its boundaries, and erasing lines. Gangubai seemed to have strains of many of these women in her, and I could see the reflection of her spirit in many of them. The story of Gangubai was also the story of all these women and the story of all these women resonated in Gangubai's life and music. Amidst yawning gaps and empty silences, there was a language—of individuals and societies at constant conflict with each other. In Gangubai, I saw the plural, multiple self, never in pursuit of self-interest. She, like all the other women, suffered, but was also capable of ending her suffering. And this was achieved through the language of her art.

Family tree

Kamalabai
had three children

a. Ambabai
had a daughter

i. Gangubai
had three children

1. Krishna

2. Babanna
has four children
a. Manoj
b. Madhavi
c. Anitha (Vaishnavi)
d. Arun

3. Narayan
has three children
a. Dinesh
b. Mahesh
c. Lakshmi

b. Krishnappa

c. Ramanna

Two favourite recipes from Gangubai

I have spent many happy hours in Gangubai's kitchen. In that warm, chaotic place, everyone would converge, talking of sundry things. I just loved to sit there, watching them operate in tandem with each other. Most of the cooking was done by Lalithakka. She sat on an old, sturdy wooden chair in front of the gas stove, and seemed to randomly throw ingredients into the pan. But it would come out with the most perfect taste.

She is truly one of the most amazing cooks I've come across.

* * *

SAMBAR

While preparing idlis for breakfast one morning, Gangubai gave me the following sambar recipe, saying: "I am not a great cook, but whatever my *maami*s taught me I learnt perfectly," she grinned.

"See … I can't specify quantities—*kannalte gottalla* (the eye decides the quantity)," she stated. She peeped into my book to make sure I was taking notes.

Ingredients:
Toor daal, channa dal
Coriander seeds
Curry leaves
Heeng
Tamarind

Jeera (cumin seeds)
Methi seeds (just a few grains)
A few peppercorns
Haldi
Red chillies
Coconut
Vegetables—carrot, bean, pea, potato, tomato and some greens
Onions
Jaggery

Method:

1. Roast the ingredients until they turn golden-brown and fill the air with a heady aroma. Run the mix in a blender until smooth.
2. Chop the vegetables fine, and pressure-cook them.
3. For seasoning, add mustard and heeng. Once the mustard splutters, sauté the onions. Now add the pressure-cooked vegetables, dal and the masala. Follow up with salt and jaggery to taste. Bring to boil.

AVALAKKI

Whenever the grandchildren came home, there would be an evening snack. Very often it would be *avalakki* (*poha*), which the children and Babanna loved. While Babanna brewed a huge vessel of tea, Lalithakka got the snack ready. There was no custom of asking "Would you like to have some?" Heads were counted and those many plates and cups were prepared.

Lalithakka is a wonderful teacher as well. Whenever she had to teach me the making of a dish, she would keep all the ingredients ready in a plate, in the right proportion. "Now, watch," she would say, sounding like a magician. Once she had taught me many different varieties of *jhunka* telling me who in the family liked which variety.

Ingredients:
Thin beaten rice
Fried gram
Cumin seeds
Heeng
Curry leaves

Chopped onions
Grated dry coconut (copra)
Lime juice
Haldi
Jaggery
Coriander leaves

Method:

1. Put oil in a pan. Throw in some grains of cumin, some heeng and curry leaves. Add finely chopped onions and fry till translucent.
2. Run the beaten rice in a mixer, allowing it to break coarsely. Put it in the pan along with fried gram powder and grated copra. Add lime juke, haldi, salt and jaggery to taste. Do not leave the pan on the flame for more than two minutes.
3. Garnish with finely chopped coriander leaves.

Acknowledgements

My association with Gangubai and her family has been a journey of trust from the word go.

Asad Zaidi of Three Essays Collective called me in 2006 after reading the piece on Gangubai Hangal I had written for the magazine *Frontline*. "Why don't you write a book?" he essayed, introducing himself. In retrospect, I believe that his was an act of remarkable trust—how do you trust someone you don't know, with a book on a legendary vocalist of national repute?

When this request was sent up to N. Ram, editor-in-chief at *The Hindu*, he sent his gracious consent in less than a day. "This is important, must be done," he had said in his email.

I was able to start work only towards the end of 2007. I made frequent trips to Hubli and, by end 2008, I realized that I couldn't go on. I had no money left: it was impossible for me to fund the project. Parvathi Menon, chief of bureau at *The Hindu*, insisted that I shouldn't stop the work. She personally drafted an application to the Directorate of Kannada and Culture, seeking a grant. From time to time she enquired about the progress of my work, and talked to me about the various processes involved. My dear friend and colleague Bhagya Prakash, who made the initial trips with me to Hubli to take photographs of the doyenne, kept me going with his keen interest in the project. Sensing my difficulty with bureaucratic red tape, my senior colleague and mentor K.N. Venkatasubba Rao generously did all the paperwork.

Deputy editor M. Baba Prasad has been a constant source of encouragement. He is among those very unusual people who remember to express happiness over a piece of writing. Even after his retirement, he called several times to say, "Don't forget to send me a copy of the book!" Our senior associate editor K. Jayant never forgot to make enquiries about the progress I was making, each time he visited Bangalore. Many thanks to the features editor Mukund Padmanabhan.

* * *

I can hardly express my indebtedness to my teacher N. Manu Chakravarthy, who was there to listen to me and advise me ever since the idea for the book came up. I am grateful to my teacher H.S. Raghavendra Rao, who read the manuscript with great care and gave me his valuable feedback. If this work merits any attention, I owe it to them and my parents, who, through their quiet ways, have conveyed to me to never steer away from the pure pursuit of things.

Without friends like K.V. Akshara not much is possible. His meticulous reading of my manuscript gave me strength.

My son Soorya has been a surprise in supporting this project. Gangubai became a strong, invisible presence in his life. He kept her glowing bright within me.

Thanks to Chitra and Ganesh.

This note would be incomplete without a mention of Dr U.R. Ananthamurthy. His interest in my work has spurred me on.

There are other friends I would like to remember—D.P. Satish came to my help, guarding me with rare affection during my trips to Delhi. My heartfelt thanks to M.R. Rakshith, Vivek Shanbhag, S. Diwakar, Girish Pattanashetty, Rishikesh Bahadur Desai, Ranjani, Bhumika, Haricharan Shenoy and Ranganath of Nudi Prakashana, who have led me through the project with their warmth.

* * *

I want to take this opportunity to remember two women, who led their lives with remarkable zest and passion. My grand-aunt Jayalakshmi Ganeshmurthy, who lost her husband early, spent all her life in Mysore teaching and performing the rare art form of *gamaka.* She remained an enthusiastic learner even at the age of eighty, and won a state honour for excellence in the field. My father's aunt Subbulakshmi was called *akka* by one and all. She lived alone in the small town of Hassan teaching Hindi, constantly engaged with a band of students and a huge community of friends and co-enthusiasts. In my growing-up years, I was awestruck by these two wonderful women who could instil the joy of learning in everyone they met. There was no trace of bitterness in them about the difficulties that life generously heaped upon them, and they always remained cheerful. My grandmothers, Jayalakshamma and Sundramma, were rare for their indomitable spirits. Jayalakshamma's love for music was moving. She could walk any distance to listen to a concert, after tending to a family of ten members. They are all long gone, but I have continuously drawn great strength from the way they lived their lives. They, in curious ways, have brought me closer to Gangubai and the women of her time.

* * *

During the course of my research, I travelled widely and met several people. I cannot recall a single bitter episode. The minute I mentioned Gangubai, doors opened and people went out of their way to help me. At the National Archives, Sangeet Natak Akademi, Gandharva Mahavidyalaya, and All India Radio, New Delhi, I obtained access to archives, documents and other research material without any glitches. How do I thank E.C. Jain, the librarian of Gandharva Mahavidyalaya, who carried the books all the way to the photocopier, there being no provision for book-lending? The seventy-year-old gentleman walked with me despite the scorching June sun of Delhi, and suggested to me articles and books that I should read. I am grateful to Dr Vageesh of All India Radio, Delhi, who had kept ready material that could be of use to me, even before I had reached. I was humbled by the effort of Sharadamma, H.Y. Sharada Prasad's wife, who, despite her multiple fractures, was sitting amidst huge piles of photographs and handwritten material from her husband's collection, and looking through them when I arrived at her apartment in Delhi late that evening. "Take everything you want. Gangubai meant a lot to us," she had offered graciously, recalling the time they had spent together.

Mr Bengeri of Sangeet Natak Akademi provided me access to their fantastic library, made arrangements to play video and audio clippings of Gangubai in the Akademi itself. I am indebted to him.

Ever since I met Susheela Ambike, Gangubai's close friend from Delhi, she became my friend as well. Susheela tai carefully tended to every question of mine in our many discussions. In Delhi, her sister Vijaya Mulay, who had made a documentary on Gangubai in the 1980s, spent a lot of time with me discussing the legendary musician and her daughter Krishna. The day I was returning, Vijaya *akka* insisted that I visit her before leaving. When I entered her house, I was told that the ninety-year-old Vijaya *akka* had gone to the market to buy sweets for me. I am filled with gratitude for all the affection that has come my way on this wonderful journey.

Dr Sadananda Kanavalli was kind enough to give me his time as well as books that would be of use to me. Not even once did Dr Patil Puttappa refuse to talk to me, though he was tied up with various commitments.

Pt. Sangameshwar Gurav, Pt. Vasant Kanakapur, Dr Prabha Atre, Pt. Prabhakar Karekar, Pt. Shripati Padegar, Pt. Chandrashekhar Puranikmath and Vaman Bendre have been generous with their inputs. I am also grateful to AIR, Dharwad. Ashok Nadiger (Gangubai's student) and Tamanna (a well-wisher of the family) have roamed with me tirelessly on the streets of Hubli, Dharwad and Kundagol. The two, being full of stories and songs, have enriched my understanding of Gangubai's story immensely. They have lavished discussions of her persona and music on me, sitting in various corners on the streets of Kundagol over many cups of tea and *mandakki.*

I simply cannot forget Jagadeesh, my Kannadiga cab-driver in Delhi. He never let me out of sight in the big, bad city. Whenever he could, he would help me with books and photocopies, carrying them as if they were his own private treasure. When Gangubai passed away, he called me from Delhi to say, "I know how sad you will be … Finish your book soon, madam."

This entire project would have collapsed without Manoj Hangal's steady support. From turning up at the railway station sleepy-eyed, to taking me around on his scooter, and making a hundred calls to people he felt I should meet, Manoj's earnestness forms the backbone of this book. His love for his grandmother is boundless.

My travel and research for this book has been partially supported by the Directorate of Kannada and Culture, Government of Karnataka, to whom I remain grateful.

This journey with Gangubai has taken me to unanticipated alleys. Her conviction has given me strength, and her goodness sans bitterness, courage. I have met the most wonderful people on this project, their passion and dedication untouched by worldly benefits. In these five years I have gained much, having seen the indomitable human spirit that endures tyranny, pain and suffering, and ventures on relentlessly.

References

Abdul Karim Khan (Hathras) [A booklet on the maestro].

Amur, G.S., *Dattatreya Ramachandra Bendre,* Makers of Indian Literature series (New Delhi, 1994).

Athavale, V.R., "A Historical Account of Marathi Stage Music," *NCPA Periodical, 7* (1978).

Bakhle, Janaki, *Two Men and Music: Nationalism in the Making of an Indian Classical Tradition* (New Delhi, 2005).

Baruah, U.L., *This is All India Radio: A Handbook of Radio Broadcasting in India* (New Delhi, 1983).

Basavanna, *Basaveshwara Vachanamruta,* edited by L. Basavaraju (1964) [Kannada].

Bendre, D.R., *Naadaleele* (Dharwad, 1972).

Bhyrappa, S.L. and Ashok Ranade, eds., *Abhinandana Grantha, Gangubai—75.*

Catlin, Amyruth, "Voice Culture: The Female Voice in the Classical Music of India and the West," *Journal of the Music Academy,* 50 (1979).

Chaudhury, Vimalakant Roy, *Bharatiya Sangeet Kosh* (New Delhi, 1975).

Comper, Denis, "A Century of Sound Recording," *The NCPA Quarterly Journal* (1988).

Deodhar, B.R., *Pillars of Hindustani Music* (Bombay, 2001).

Deshpande, Vamanrao, "AIR obituary for Sawai Gandharva" (1952) [Marathi].

—— *Between Two Tanpuras* (Bombay, 1989).

—— "Sawai Gandharv," *Journal of Sangeet Kala Vihar* (1952).

Devi, Savita and Vibha Chauhan, *Maa ... Siddeshwari* (New Delhi, 2000).

Dhaneshwar, Amarendra, "Remembering Hirabai," *Sangeet Natak* (New Delhi).

Dhar, Sheila, *Raga'n Josh: Stories from a Musical Life* (New Delhi, 2005).

Gandhi, M.K., *Diet and Diet Reform* (Ahmedabad, 1949).

Gupta, Sahana, *Ustad Alauddin Khan* (Delhi, 2009).

Hiranand, Shanti, *Begum Akhtar: The Story of My Ammi* (New Delhi, 2005).

Joshi, G.N., *Down Melody Lane* (Bombay, 1984).

Joshi, Naveen, *Aspects of Indian Music* (New Delhi, 1970).

Joshi, Shirish, *Kumar Gandharva,* (Belgaum, 2005) [Kannada].

Kanavalli, Sadananda, *Karnataka's Hindustani Musicians* (New Delhi, 2004).

—— *Mallikarjun Mansur* (Gadag, 1992) [Kannada].

—— *Sawai Gandharva* (Gadag).

Karnani, Chetan, *Form in Indian Music: A Study in Gharanas* (Jaipur, 2005).

—— *Listening to Indian Music* (New Delhi, 1999).

Khot, Dr Jayant, "Abdul Karim Khan and His Thumri," *Journal of Sangeet Kala Vihar* (1997).

Kothari, Sunil, "History: Roots, Growth and Revival," in *Bharata Natyam: Indian Classical Dance Art* (New Delhi, 1979).

Kulkarni, N.K., *Dattatreya Ramachandra Bendre* (Bangalore) [Published by Navakarnataka in Kannada].

Lakshmi, C.S., *The Singer and the Song* (New Delhi, 2000).

Majumdar, Abhik, *Bhimsen Joshi: A Passion for Music* (New Delhi, 2004).

Mansur, Mallikarjun, *Nanna Rasayaatre* (1981) Bangalore, [Kannada].

Marulkar, Dr N.R. and Shantadevi Marulkar, *Sangeet Ke Gharane* (1986) [Hindi].

Mayor, Geeta, "Homage to Bhatkhande".

Menon, Indira, *Great Masters of Carnatic Music: 1930-1965* (New Delhi, 2007).

Menon, Raghava, *Indian Music: The Magic of the Raga* (Mumbai, 1998).

Misra, Susheela, *Some Immortals of Hindustani Music* (New Delhi, 1990).

Mishra, Amar Prasad, *Some Musical Memories* (New Delhi, 2004).

Mukherji, Kumar Prasad, *The Lost World of Hindustani Music* (New Delhi, 2006).

Mulagunda, Arvind, ed., *Pandit Bhimsen Joshi* (Bangalore, 2010) [Kannada].

Nadkarni, Mohan, *Bhimsen Joshi: A Biography* (New Delhi, 1993).

—— *The Great Masters: Profiles in Hindustani Classical Vocal Music* (New Delhi, 1999).

Nag, Dipali, *Ustad Faiyaaz Khan* (New Delhi, 1985).

Narasimhan, Sakuntala, *The Splendour of Rampur-Sahaswan Gharana: Of Hindustani Music, Its Evolution, History, Characteristics and Compositions* (Bangalore, 2006).

Nayar, Sobhana, *Bhatkhande's Contribution to Music: A Historical Perspective* (Bombay, 1987).

Parthasarathy, T.S., "Bhatkhande and Paluskar," *The Journal of the Music Academy,* 50 (1979).

Potdar, Vasanta, *Bheemasena* (Dharwad, 2006) [Kannada].

Presidential Address of Dr. T. Balasaraswati at the 33rd Annual Conference of the Tamil Isai Sangam, Madras, 21 December 1975.

Raja, Deepak, *Hindustani Music: A Tradition in Transition* (New Delhi, 2004).

—— *Khayal Vocalism: Continuity Within Change* (New Delhi, 2009).

Raman, N. Pattabhi and Anandhi Ramachandran, "T. Balasaraswati: The Whole World in Her Hands," *Sangeet Natak,* 72-3 (1984).

Ranade, Ashok D., *On Music and Musicians of Hindoostan* (New Delhi, 1984).

—— *Stage Music of Maharashtra* (New Delhi, 1986).

—— *Hindustani Music* (New Delhi, 1997).

Said, Edward W., *Music At the Limits* (New York, 2007).

Salt, Henry Stephens, *A Plea for Vegetarianism and Other Essays* (Manchester, 1886).

Sampath, Vikram, *Splendours of Royal Mysore: The Untold Story of the Wodeyars* (New Delhi, 2008).

Sankaran, T., *Bangalore Nagaratnamma: A Devadasi True.*

Seth, Niharika, *Ustad Vilayat Khan: A Life Set to Music* (New Delhi, 2004).

Showalter, Elaine, *A Literature of Their Own: British Women Novelists from Brontë to Lessing* (Princeton, 1977).

Sriram, V., *The Devadasi and the Saint: The Life and Times of Bangalore Nagarathnamma,* (Chennai, 2007).

Subramanian, Lakshmi, *Veena Dhanammal: The Making of a Legend* (London and New York, 2009).

Takar, Sulabha, "Kirana Gharana Ki Gayaki—Laya Ke Sandharbh Mein," *Journal of Sangeet Kala Vihar* (Solapur, 1984) [Hindi].

Tharu, Susie and K. Lalita, *Women Writing in India: 600 BC to the Present, i: 600 BC to the Early Twentieth Century* (New York, 1991).

The Great Masters: Hirabai Badodekar [Special Issue], *Sangeet Natak* (New Delhi).

Thieme, John and Ira Raja, eds., *The Table Is Laid: The Oxford Anthology of South Asian Food Writing* (New Delhi, 2007).

Weidman, Amanda J., *Singing the Classical, Voicing the Modern: The Postcolonial Politics of Music in South India* (Calcutta, 2006).

Williams, Howard, *The Ethics of Diet: An Anthology of Vegetarian Thought* (Guildford Surrey, 2010).

Index